The Nearby Faraway

The Nearby Faraway

A Personal Journey
through the Heart of the West

David Petersen

FOREWORD BY ANN ZWINGER

Johnson Books

BOULDER

COVER

"Thoreau at the Cabin"
wood engraving by Michael McCurdy (1985)

"Though the view from my door was ... contracted, I did not
feel crowded or confined in the least. There was pasture enough
for my imagination. The low shrub-oak plateau to which the
opposite shore arose, stretched away toward the prairies of the
West. ..."   —from *Walden*

Published in the United States by Johnson Books, a division of Johnson Publishing
Company, 1880 South 57th Court, Boulder, Colorado 80301.

9   8   7   6   5   4   3   2

Cover illustration: Michael McCurdy
Cover design: Debra B. Topping

Chapter 6 from *Ghost Grizzlies*, by David Petersen. Copyright © 1995 by David Petersen.
Reprinted by permission of Henry Holt & Co., Inc.

Library of Congress Cataloging-in-Publication Data
Petersen, David, 1946–
    The nearby faraway: a personal journey through the heart of the
West / by David Petersen; foreword by Ann Zwinger.
        p.   cm.
        ISBN 1-55566-206-4 (cloth: alk. paper)—ISBN 1-55566-187-4
(pbk.: alk. paper)
        1. Rocky Mountains—Description and travel. 2. West (U.S.)—
Description and travel. 3. Natural history—Rocky Mountains.
4. Natural history—West (U.S.) 5. Petersen, David, 1946– .
I. Title.
F721.P48 1997
917.804'33—dc 21   97-28206
                                                              CIP

Printed in the United States by
Johnson Printing
1880 South 57th Court

 Printed on recycled paper with soy ink

Contents

For Caroline

In my imagination, through ways incomprehensible to the author, desire and love and death lead through the wilderness of human life into the wilderness of the natural world—and continue, round and round, perhaps forever, back again to wherever it is we began.

—*Edward Abbey*

Foreword

GATHERING A COLLECTION of one's essays is not an easy task. When a writer puts together essays written over a period of time, he becomes the proverbial drowning man, observing his life and work pass before his eyes. He also assumes a split identity. He is first person singular: I wrote this, I remember the rustle of leaves, the smell of mushrooms on a wet morning, the catch of breath at danger, the last sunset, each essay, each experience seen alone as it was originally written. But he is also third person singular: what, editorially, should be included, how does each essay take on a different meaning in the context of adjacent essays rather than being seen alone as it was originally written.

The examination of time and place, where and when, is a necessary examination that can be gratifying as well as unsettling. There is the inevitable confrontation with self: impossible ever to look upon an essay as perfection, as an end-all, and yet there are satisfactions in a well-turned phrase and a recognition of how the years have been spent that offer, especially in a profession as solitary as writing, a pleasure in how one's time has been spent.

David Petersen's essays are for those of us who, at one time or another, have wanted to get away from it all, maybe even step into someone else's life-style and mind, to cruise the shores of different ideas, and make landfall at new realizations. If not, they are even more for you.

Petersen is an uncommonly good writer and a very good observer, able to enrich and embroider an idea or experience. He has a well-grounded philosophy of life, built on experience, and whether it is yours or not, challenges you as a reader to take stock of where you stand vis-à-vis this world of ours. You can take comfort from the words of someone who lives by his ideas and ideals, quietly and tactfully, one who lives *with* the landscape.

He can make getting away from it all possible through vivid landscape description, new ideas to hold hands with and, best of all, return you to your own life refreshed and smiling. The sincerity and competence of the skilled outdoorsman revitalize an armchair reader. For Petersen *lives* out there and cherishes the privilege, remembers the immensity and the minutia, honors the aspen tree.

His essays chronicle a great love of the particular place he lives in the Colorado mountains, a love affair with grizzly bears, facing death and loving life, as well as affection and loyalty for friends and colleagues. In other words, the verities. The things we don't stop to think about enough. The real world.

His last line, "I have no choice," is touching and true, a desperately quiet recognition of the necessity of his life's work. In many lives, that often means being trapped; in Petersen's life, it means he is grounded, he knows where he's coming from and where he's going, and "no choice" gives him the freedom to pursue an esoteric profession in the most professional and moving way possible. He personifies Gary Snyder's lines, "Stay together/Learn the flowers/Go light."

"I have no choice." For that, may we all be joyful.

Ann Zwinger
COLORADO SPRINGS, COLORADO

PART ONE

❧

At Home
Among the Aspens

1

In the Nearby Faraway

I'M MOVING QUIETLY through a parklike grove of quaking aspens in the San Juan Mountains of southwestern Colorado, a couple of miles from my year-round home. I've come here, like so many evenings before, simply to see what I can see.

Not wanting to disturb the tranquillity of this special place—this Nearby Faraway (with apologies to Georgia O'Keeffe)—I'm dressed in camouflage and doing my best to keep my movements as slow as the progress of time and as quiet as ... what? As quiet as a stumbling, bumbling, middle-aged human can manage.

Just ahead, a predictably ill-tempered *Perisoreus canadensis*—a large, white-crowned, black-tipped gray bird known commonly and variously as the gray jay, Canada jay, Whiskey Jack and, the most accurate of its many *noms de plume*, camp robber—screams a harsh familiar alarm then drops from its lofty perch, strokes hard on noisy wings and sails away, tilting low amongst the stark, standing beams of the aspen forest.

This minor commotion in turn startles to flight a pair of sweet-voiced chickadees. What a beautifully onomatopoetical name, that one, given the little gray-and-white bird's distinct, repetitive call of *Chicka-dee-dee-dee.*

Up the valley a ways, hard to say exactly how far, an autumn-enamored bull elk issues a drawn-out bugle, bluesy as Beal Street, like a three-octave run of bent high notes on a saxophone. With the wolf exterminated from Colorado the same year I was born, and the loon not indigenous to these parts, the elk—or, more properly,

3

wapiti (Shawnee for "white rump")—is nature's wildest surviving Colorado voice. I wait impatiently for eleven months every year to hear that pagan music, and live daily with the troubling knowledge that should it ever go missing from these wilds, something vital in me will have died with it.

I move on, even more slowly and carefully now, following a dim game trail that twists and dodges through the aspens, hoping to catch a glimpse of the bugling bull; these are not half-tamed park animals, and making a close approach is difficult if not impossible.

I step ever so cautiously, stopping often to look, listen and savor the wild familiar scents floating my way on the downslope evening breeze: the tangy, pungent smell of autumn aspens; the heavy barnyard funk of bull wapiti in lust; and the fresh, willowy aroma rising from the small spring pool that waters this tight little valley with its canopy of aspen, ponderosa pine, spruce and fir understoried with pine drops the color of dried blood, ladyferns both common and alpine, giant larkspur and cow parsnips, chokecherry, serviceberry, bearberry, wild raspberry, columbines red and blue and other lush living things whose names I'll not likely live long enough to learn.

The ground and vegetation here are moist, making the going quiet, easy. This advantage, however, is offset by a jungle of undergrowth so profuse that I can see no more than a few yards in any direction.

Suddenly, from out of a brushy tangle of Gambel's oak just ahead, an animal appears: roundish, the color of milk chocolate, the size more or less of a badger but much too furry and fat for that. What it is, I realize with a start, is a bear cub, small for so late in the season but a bear cub nonetheless. I am surprised, elated—and a little concerned.

Now a second cub, a twin to the first, comes shambling out of the same scrubby island of brush. And a third. And all three are wobbling my way.

Notwithstanding the considerable amount of time I spend alone in this aspen grove and many similar others, and even given the generous black bear population hereabouts, my close-up bruin sightings this season have been, as they say, few and far between. The appearance of this wee trio is great good luck. Yet I'm distracted by one nigglesome worry: *Where might their mother be?*

The sow doesn't keep me waiting and wondering for long, making a silent entrance through a curtain of aspen saplings thirty yards or so up the valley. Thank the gods she's upwind.

Hump-shouldered and autumn fat, this little female is by far the most beautifully marked specimen of *Ursus americanus* I've ever encountered, more closely resembling a runted grizzly than your average black bear. Most significantly, she isn't black. Her legs, head and ample rump are patched over with the same Hershey brown that completely clothes her cubs, but across her back is draped a broad shawl of straw blond. And all of her is mottled with a shifting pattern of light and shadow as she moves beneath the scattered shafts of low-angle evening sunlight fingering down through the quakies.

The sow browses slowly toward me—relaxed, undisturbed, as such an encounter should be—gobbling wildflowers, nipping cow parsnips, scratching bemusedly at the dark moist soil, looking for who knows what. Insouciant, beautiful.

Rooted here like a hoary old pine snag amidst her swarming brood of cubs, it strikes me that this encounter is a potentially mixed blessing. I know, intellectually at least, there's little to worry about, that black bears almost never act aggressively toward humans. Almost never, that is, so long as they're treated with the respect due unto the large, fast, heavily muscled, well-armed, unpredictable, opportunistic predatory wild beasts they are. Truly wild black bears, those that live outside the protective bounds of parks and preserves and have been spared familiarization with people and addiction to people's food, are among the most reclusive of all large North American mammals, wanting only to be left alone and almost always turning stubby tail to run from the slightest hint of human intrusion. That's why black bears are so rarely seen, even where both they and people abound, and why they have survived and prospered where the more aggressive and visible grizzly has not.

Yet, I also know that in the past century several dozen people have been mauled by black bears and more than two dozen killed. Worse, a handful of those attacks were determined (by the most grisly evidence imaginable) to have been predacious—the bears, for whatever reasons, had come to view humans (often but not always children) as prey. One singularly unfortunate and incredibly courageous Canadian woman, after being viciously attacked by a predacious black bear, lay as if dead while the beast slowly ate both her arms. Miraculously, she was rescued just in time to live to tell about it.

But *stop it;* why am I thinking these paranoid thoughts?

The mind works in weird ways when under acute pressure. At least mine does. Just now for instance, standing here knee-deep in baby bears, the tree-top rattle of sere autumn aspen leaves reminds me that another summer has come and all but gone. Fall is upon us and winter is just over the proverbial hill. That's no doubt why this bruin family is out and about in daylight, rather than awaiting the anonymity of darkness to venture abroad; they're maximizing the brief remaining time before the snows come, embarked on a last-ditch fattening spree in anticipation of the rapidly approaching denning season.

Thinking about the extreme cold and overwhelming depths of snow that freeze-frame this high corrugated country for a good four or more months of winter each year, I'm led to wonder where these bears will hole up. Perhaps right here in this enchanted aspen valley? Within the hollowed bole of some long-dead forest giant? Beneath the shelter of an overhanging rock ledge? In a laboriously dug earthen den? Or merely in a natural depression, such as created when a heavily rooted tree topples, with the snow alone to hide and insulate them?

With no apparent provocation, the cub nearest me suddenly sprints up a skinny young aspen, then looks to see if his siblings will follow. They don't, and the disappointed climber soon shinnies back down, demonstrating an apparently natural-born talent for sylvan acrobatics.

Natural-born talent, yes, but the skill still must be practiced and mastered. Among the first lessons any right-minded bear mother teaches a new brood of cubs after leading them from their nursery den in May is the high art of tree climbing. Very young black bears are defenseless when away from their mother, and—as evidenced by the trio frolicking even now around my boots—are filled with the reckless abandon of youth. Were it not for their ability and eager willingness to climb trees, first-year bear cubs almost certainly would fall prey to coyotes, cougars, adult male bears and other predators far more often than they do.

I cautiously shift my gaze from the cubs back to their mother. The sow continues to narrow the distance between us and is now only twenty yards up the valley; not nearly far enough. Time to consider my options. Such as they are.

Moving only my eyes, I survey the trees around me, sizing them up for climbability. Discounting one huge ponderosa pine, a high-limbed monster much too fat to wrap my limbs around, all the trees within my grasp are smooth-barked aspens, and none have limbs (those enticing projections that desperate folk are wont to go out on) low enough to grab and haul myself up by. Adding the promise of injury to insult, fully a quarter of the aspens surrounding me wear on their pale skins the rough, dark scars of old wounds inflicted by the short, heavy claws of climbing bears. Not just cubs, but adult blacks as well are superb climbers. My flee-up-a-tree option, alas, is bankrupt.

The cubs continue to romp nearby. The sow feeds ever closer.

Mounting a viable self-defense seems equally unlikely. For one thing, I like bears, whether they care for me or not. Besides, the hunting knife I pack along on all solo treks into the backcountry (a carbon steel talisman against all manner of emergencies, imagined and real) is beyond immediate reach, thrust deep into the bowels of the day pack riding on my back. And just as well, I guess, since I don't feel much like becoming a contemporary Hugh Glass—a gritty 1820s mountain man who attempted to defend himself with a knife after being attacked by an out-of-sorts mother grizzly, only to spend the next several weeks gimping around the boonies with a body like Swiss cheese.

But all is not lost: As close as she is, the sow is still upwind of me and preoccupied with stuffing her face. But it won't be long before she catches on. It *can't* be much longer now, near as she is. Bears may or may not be the weak-eyed creatures they're often said to be, but even sharp-sighted animals have a hard time distinguishing a stationary object from its background, and I'm fully camouflaged. Yet, bears' ears are keen and their noses are unsurpassed in all of nature.

Considering the iffy hand I've been dealt here, it's obvious that my best—perhaps my *only*—bet to avoid being transmogrified into fresh bear plop is to stand pat until the danger has passed—or until the sow detects me, decides that I'm a threat to her cubs and calls in the cards with a huffing charge. At which time I'll either stoically stand my ground, avert my eyes and speak calmly to the bear in an attempt to assure her I'm no threat to her young—or (more likely) panic and attempt, pointless though it may be, to wing it up the nearest aspen, there to tremble in company with the timid yellow leaves.

As the trio of cubs continues to romp nearby, circling me as if I were some weird two-legged maypole, and their well-clawed mother grunts and grazes steadily nearer, I strain to remain motionless and to slow the Gatling-gun beating of my heart.

Thus we approach the denouement. In the recounting, if not in the actual unfolding of this small adventure, I long for a calamitous climax: The sudden discovery ... the growling, teeth-clacking charge ... my heroic and miraculous escape.

But, alas, mere fact must suffice. The sow, like most females I meet in passing, simply cruises right on by without giving me even so much as a sidelong glance.

Then, downwind by fifty yards or so, the adult bear suddenly spins around and bawls. At this urgent signal, her three cubs dash to her furry flanks. Obviously, she has finally intercepted my scent wake and—typically, wisely—chosen flight over fight. I watch and listen, relief mixed with sorrow, as the hirsute family shuffles down the valley and out of my life, probably forever.

A few moments more and my bears are gone, shadowy forms swallowed by the sheltering forest.

2

Wild Things

THE GAME TRAIL, ancient and dim yet clearly discernible to an attentive eye, angles down across a steep, south-facing hill grown thick in aspen, pine, fir, spruce and scrubby Gambel's oak.

Near the base of the hill the trail passes close by a deformed old ponderosa pine whose thick, twisted lower trunk emulates the graceful curves of a swan's neck—a deformity suffered, no doubt, when the tree was young and malleable and had the misfortune of being bent under a winter's weight of snow, or perhaps a fallen older brother. But like all living beings with spine and character, the swan tree overcame its disadvantage and today reaches for the sky with the best of them.

From the swan tree, the old game trail ambles obliquely on down the hill, snaking through a dense understory of oak, chokecherry, bearberry, wild rose and other woody browse.

At its base, the hill meets a gentler slope that drops off to the west for a distance of a couple hundred yards down to the bottom of a narrow valley carrying a thin perennial stream—a stream that begins up high in a place called Missionary Ridge (so-named, says local legend, because it reminded an emigrant from Tennessee of that infamous Civil War battleground). Here, where south-facing hill meets west-facing slope, the old game trail forks, forks again and finally dissipates amongst a grove of mixed-age quaking aspens.

As the old trail suggests, for decades (at the very least) this hillside quakie stand has been a haven for wildlife, in particular deer, elk and bears. Alas, only blackies remain these emasculated days, though hold-out grizzlies roamed hereabouts less than twenty years ago. The animal officially hailed as the last Colorado grizzly was killed in hand-to-claw combat with a hunter in September of 1979. That historic drama played itself out just fifty-seven arrow-flight miles southwest of here.

Everything needed by the indigenous wild creatures that for so long followed the old game trail into this hillside aspen haven remains abundant hereabouts: pure, reliable water in the creek just down the way; a lush understory of brush, tall grasses and wildflowers on which to feed and among which to rest hidden from danger; leafy trees for thermal cover; food aplenty, with virtually every under-story plant that grows here edible to herbivorous elk and deer, omnivorous bears and many another wild thing; and, as an important bonus, especially for elk, when times get really tough (as they do most every winter), are the nutritious sprouting limbs and leaf-buds of oak and aspen, as well as the green, living inner bark of the latter—wapiti survival rations.

This special place—this little hillside aspen grove with the worn and timeless game trail wandering through it—is my front yard.

Evidence of wildlife having used this aspen grove abounds: Standing like ivory pillars on either side of my front door are a bone-white brace of mature quakies, both of which boast the time-blackened scars of climbing ursines; age-blackened bear tracks ascending white bark. Other aspens nearby wear the distinctive long, curving scars left by porcupines—whose primary food is the under-bark of conifers, but who nonetheless occasionally climb aspens, especially saplings, to eat their soft green cambium. And hardly an adult quakie hereabouts has escaped the wintertime nibbling of elk, evidenced by distinct rows of tooth scars on the trunks, beginning near the ground and extending several feet up. Likewise, the deeply gouged scars of autumn antler rubs, both deer and elk, are ubiquitous.

All of this, and more, is irrefutable proof that this place—back before it was unlucky enough to get itself roaded and settled—was prime wildlife habitat.

Have Caroline and I, merely by being here, robbed local wild creatures of the use of this place? Well, yes and no. Yes, in a general sense, insofar as our very presence—the presence of any humans with our carnivorous pets, our obtrusive buildings, our infernal machines with their stink and noise—displaces and frightens and keeps wildlife at a distance. But in a more personal sense, no, in that one of the reasons we chose to put down on this particular mountainside is that it had been subdivided and roaded long before our arrival; the greater damage had long since been done.

And no, also, insofar as Caroline and I (and a rare few others among our scattered neighbors) take every precaution to make certain that our presence creates as little disturbance to the natural world as possible. Unlike some, we have not converted our little acreage into a graveled parking lot, a domestic menagerie or a trash dump, and we do not feel the urban refugees' uneasy need to flood the rural night with the harsh intrusion of outdoor lighting. We *like* the company of our wild friends, including their occasional spooky bumps in the night, and if they fail to reciprocate in these feelings at least they seem not to fear or avoid us unduly.

In fact, it was the animals themselves who first revealed to me their ancestral path winding down off the hillside.

ॐ

One September morning several years ago, while sitting at my plywood-plank desk scribbling (then as now), I caught a glimpse of movement out the window to my front. I looked up to see one, two, three mule deer bucks inching down the hill toward the cabin. The first was a yearling with unforked "spike" antlers. Behind him came a fork-horn (two points per side). And bringing up the rear was a high-antlered three-pointer. On came the horny bachelor party, passing close by the swan tree, on down past the water well and out into the aspens just twenty yards from my window, where they began to nip and browse.

I stood from my desk, slipped to the front door, eased it open. But the largest buck spotted even this small, slow movement, or perhaps he heard the barely audible squeak of the door hinges, and snapped to attention: head and tail up, ears swiveled forward, body rigid. I stood motionless in the doorway, and after a short while the sentry relaxed and returned to nibbling selectively at brush and saplings—including the tops of four young fruit trees Caroline had recently planted. The cropped trees eventually succumbed to this harsh pruning, but, at least from my point of view (I can't speak for the trees), the encounter was worth the loss.

After the deer had gone, browsing on down the hill and out of sight, I backtracked them and discovered the old trail, its dim outline highlighted in yellow by fallen autumn aspen leaves and packed with fresh deer prints. How long had I lived here without noticing it? Too long.

Another time, during our first fall here, I hiked far up the mountain and killed a yearling bull elk for winter meat. After quartering the carcass and packing it down with the help of a neighbor and a borrowed mule named Hercules (and that he was), I boned, butchered and wrapped the meat for the freezer. What remained of the skeleton—the spinal column with ribs still attached—I hung from a young aspen near the cabin. In my beginner's ignorance, I wanted to see what would happen.

A bear came that very night, and the next, biting clean through the heavy bones and completely devouring the meaty skeleton. All that remained was the claw-scarred, blood- and tallow-smeared aspen from which the offering had hung. Older and perhaps somewhat wiser now, I know that such innocent "baiting" is a dangerous mistake, a tragedy in the making. The last thing any rural resident should be doing, especially in the fall, is luring bears into the yard with ani-

mal carcasses, garbage, pet food or any other smelly edibles. A fed
bear is a dead bear.

But back then, Caroline and I enjoyed our ingenuousness to the
hilt, and nothing untoward came of it. At least so far as we ever knew.
It's doubtful, however, that the unfortunate young quakie shared our
affection for the bear's visit. In the process of her unmannered feeding, the bear excoriated the slender tree of its soft, living bark from
the ground to about six feet up. Although not entirely girdled and
thus killed outright, with each passing year the bear-bared tree has
grown less vigorous, its severely damaged skin hardening, blackening
and drawing away from the trunk in big scabrous slabs, becoming a
haven for insects and the hammer-headed birds that sound them out
and eat them.

Woodpeckers, in fact, know of the impending death of an aspen
well before any mere human—or even, I suspect, the tree itself—ever
could. It is late spring now, and the summer's new leaves are unfurling on the bear-damaged aspen, offering an optimistic hope of continued life. And even as I scrawl these scattered thoughts a hairy
woodpecker busies herself filching sunflower seeds from the nearby
feeder and depositing them—hoarding, I suppose, for the always-
coming winter—under the loose slabs of blackened bark and in
dozens of small deep holes she has drilled into the pulpy trunk of the
ailing tree. The bird would not do this if the tree were healthy. Come
fall, I fear, the bear-clawed aspen is destined for the woodpile. For this
I feel responsible, and I am sorry.

~

Woodpeckers—in particular the hairy and downy models, along
with their vociferous cousin the red-shafted flicker—are important
members of the aspen community. All are primary cavity builders—
species that excavate nesting holes in dead and diseased (and, thus,

soft-cored) trees. In fact, each female woodpecker, apparently just for the sheer joy of doing what the species does best, excavates several aspen cavities each season, from which will be selected just one as a nursery den. But there is little waste in nature, with the excess 'pecker holes quickly being occupied by such secondary cavity dwellers as small owls, swallows and other birds, and tree squirrels.

One summer a few years ago, I was mildly miffed when a hairy woodpecker drilled into a big handsome aspen standing a couple dozen yards from our kitchen window, and promptly moved in. My anger cooled when, some time later, a single chick appeared.

The chick quickly grew to a size almost equal its mother, and we enjoyed monitoring its daily routine: When the mother was out hunting, the fledgling would abide quietly within the safety of its woody cavity—listening, waiting—only occasionally sticking its head out to reconnoiter. But the moment the adult appeared, and before it even landed (I assume the young one heard her approach, though I never could), the chick would thrust its head and fluffy breast out of the hole and beg shrilly until fed. Occasionally, the youngster would mistake human voices or the sounds of our rustling around outside for its mother, and make a cacophonous appearance.

Unfortunately, we missed the moment of the chick's first flight and departure, and were sorry to discovery one fine summer's day that both it and its mom had gone.

Not long after, I used a ladder to climb up and explore the abandoned nest hole. The entrance was about the diameter and shape of a chicken egg, opening into a cavity the size of a large grapefruit. It was during this postpartum exploration that I discovered that the nest tree, while fully leafed and apparently healthy, was in fact punky inside—another silent victim of heartrot. The woodpecker had known what I would never have guessed, since the tree showed no outward ill symptoms.

Even though woodpeckers may damage the occasional healthy

aspen, they no doubt do far more good than bad, feeding heavily on the larva and adult forms of various harmful insects, including the deadly poplar borer (genus *Saperda*).

Caroline and I are happy to share "our" aspens with the 'peckers and their flighty avian kin. The latter include, according to season, mourning doves, band-tailed pigeons (a rare sweet treat), blue grouse, wild turkeys (Merriam's subspecies), hawks, falcons, owls (notably the great horned), an occasional aloof golden (summer) or bald (fall and winter) eagle, "nighthawks" (*Chordeiles minor*) and a myriad of summertime songbirds (chickadees, nuthatches, pygmy nuthatches, Steller's jays, grosbeaks, flycatchers, pine siskins and three brands of junco).

Come winter, most of these happy summer singers fly the coop, so to speak, leaving the silent groves to the hardiest of their number and the occasional large mammal.

For an instance: On two consecutive nights last March a band of elk (too few to call a herd) visited the oak tangle just a stone's toss up the hill. Both nights, when I stepped outside to water the dog, several of the giant deer (*Cervus elaphus,* for those who care about such things) crunched around nervously up there on the frozen snow, waiting, albeit impatiently, for us to finish our business and go back inside. But the elk did not run, nor even bark (a loud, sharp, very doglike sound that is the elk alarm call). They know us. They trust us. They have to if they want to utilize the local oak brush and the bark and twigs of our front-yard aspens for winter browse.

Come spring, both elk and deer feed heavily on the budding tops of aspen saplings. The quakie is truly a wildlife food for all seasons— just as it has become rich spiritual food for me.

Of course, other wild creatures besides elk consume the bark, buds and branch tips of quaking aspens. Even the porcupine—that familiar large prickly rodent generally thought to prefer the bark of conifers and the rubber of automobile radiator hoses—occasionally feeds on aspen, consuming the green leaves in summer and the bark and buds in winter. Several years ago, a single hungry porky wiped out an entire little clutch of aspen saplings growing close by the cabin, stripping every shred of accessible bark from the little trees—from their tips right down to snow level—in a single night. Not a pretty sight.

And then there are the bears. In spring, soon after emerging from den, with a hunger for green stuff working deep within, black bears climb mature aspens to break off limbs for their abundant buds and catkins and, a little later, new leaves. When a sufficient pile of limbs litters the ground beneath the dinner tree, the bear descends to feed. And so on.

But the mammal most closely associated with aspens—in fact, it shares with them a symbiotic (mutually beneficial and dependent) relationship—is the beaver. Not only is aspen the beaver's food of first choice, it's also the preferred building material for this biggest North American rodent's wigwam homes and the log-and-mud dams that create its own private waterworld.

In the fall, by way of storing up for winter, the toothy rodents stay busy as a you-know-what cutting aspen branches—dragging them in from as far abroad as three hundred yards and occasionally farther, though most cutting activity is restricted to three hundred feet around the shores—and anchoring them to the bottoms of their ponds. When snow covers the land and surface ice seals the ponds, the beautifully evolved aquatic mammals simply slip into the frigid water through ports in the floors of their lodges and swim down to retrieve a cold-preserved aspen salad.

The average adult beaver will consume a little over four pounds of aspen bark per day—some fifteen hundred pounds per year—preferring to peel its dinner from relatively small-diameter trees and limbs, downing perhaps as many as two hundred trees in the doing. Such gluttonous consumption is the equivalent of clearcutting within reach of the beaver pond.

In the short run, this all seems pretty one-way in the beaver's favor:

The rodent fells aspens, strips and eats their bark and twigs then uses the peeled limbs and trunks to build its dams and lodges. So how is the relationship symbiotic? In the long view: Beavers build the dams that form the ponds that eventually dry up and become sedge marshes then meadows and finally renewed aspen groves.

Of course, it takes awhile—from a dozen or so years up to centuries, depending on local circumstances—for a good crop of aspen saplings to reappear in a beaver-cut area. But whether perceived as good, bad or indifferent, the beaver—with its rich fur, webbed feet, oversized choppers, big flat tail, stick dams, interlocking stepped pond systems, bank tunnels, mud slides, island lodges, acres of pointed aspen stumps and Protestant workaholic ethic—is inseparable in most knowledgeable observers' minds from the healthy aspen forest.

Fact is, the Rockies just wouldn't be the Rockies were they devoid of their thousands of beaver ponds, the sleek brown heads of the busy builders cutting the evening surface as they swim, parting the dark glassy water with ever-broadening Vs, like widening waves of tranquillity.

Even so, I do sometimes wish the fiercely territorial beasts weren't quite so persistent in swimming up to anglers and tail-slapping the water—*Blam! Blam!*—like so many shotgun blasts. For the beavers, the slap is merely a territorial warning. But for the angler who may have hiked miles to a favorite trout pond while suffering swarms of mosquitoes en route, and who means the residents thereof no harm (not even the trout), and no matter how highly he may otherwise regard the beaver, the sound of one tail slapping equals the sound of no fish caught.

Without doubt, the most harmful animals to the aspen ecology over the long haul are not beavers, not woodpeckers or any other wild things, but domestic cattle and sheep. Particularly the latter. According to a U.S. Forest Service study: "When grazed at similar intensities, sheep were four times more destructive to aspen suckers [saplings] than cattle. ... After the impact of livestock, the additional impact of elk scattered over their summer range is seldom even measurable."

The management implications are clear: In order to maintain a healthy aspen ecology that can support itself in addition to an abundance of dependent life (mine humbly included), livestock grazing must be strictly limited and carefully monitored.

For this reason and many good others (the destruction of riparian habitat and the consequent watershed damage; severe overgrazing leading to soil dehydration and desertification; the government-sponsored slaughter of natural predators; and so on, and on), many informed and (thus) concerned Americans feel strongly that livestock grazing should be eliminated from public lands. Or at least more closely regulated.

The key players, of course—those with vested interests in public lands livestock grazing and other forms of totalitarian agriculture, notably the BLM (Bureau of Livestock Mismanagement), the U.S. Forest Service, the professional predator killers of the U.S. Department of Agriculture's Animal Damage Control branch and of course the ranchers themselves—are always vocal and (the latter two at least) occasionally forceful in their disagreement. (For speaking my views in public, I've been threatened with arrest, with litigation and even with being "taken care of." The latter is good news indeed, given that I have no insurance, no savings and often wonder who will care for me in my dotage.)

The village dogs bark, the caravan moves on ... of course, of course. The question is—where to from here?

3

Autumn Aspen Haiku

DURING ALL THE young years I suffered in cities, like most others who spend more time walking on concrete than bare earth, I counted the turning of the seasons by calendar pages and the passing of holidays. Since coming here to the Rockies, I've learned to look beyond human temporal constructs and rely on nature as my seasonal calendar: Springtime begins the day the winter's snow has melted sufficiently to allow the first spring beauties (*claytonia*) to flower, and becomes official when the quakie catkins burst and the robins return and start stabbing at the moist snowmelt soil for sluggish April earthworms.

Summer arrives on the wings of scarlet-and-yellow western tanagers; the shy, nervous mourning dove; the graceful nighthawk with its darting flight, daring dives and whooshing sonic booms; the renewal of the mosquitoes upon which the nighthawks feed; and, most significantly, the leafing of the aspens.

Autumn (that saddest and most sublime of seasons) is heralded by the brassy bugling of rutting bull elk and painted across the hillsides by the dying leaves of aspens. As early as mid-August, yellow leaves begin dotting the ground, though no visible sign of change is apparent in the lime-green canopies above. By month's end, however, the early turners are doing their thing; spreading splotches of gold across the green hillsides, and one of the most beautiful processes in nature has begun. Given favorable conditions (namely, a lack of wind storms and driving rain or hail), this golden glory can linger well into October.

But there's no waste in nature, and the benefits to the ecology of the annual aspen leaf crop don't end with their short working lives. When the leaves dry, detach and float to the ground, they become part of a rich mulch, or duff, that quickly decomposes and returns stored nutrients to the soil. Additionally, aspen leaves—both living and fallen—help to feed some three hundred species of invertebrates, thus facilitating the transition from vegetable to flesh and providing a strong foundation link in the forest food chain.

Finally and inevitably, winter begins with a diving thermometer and the first major snowfall, bleaching the mountains of their residual brilliance and stripping the quakies to naked skeletons. Thus is recited the annual ...

AUTUMN ASPEN HAIKU
Yellow leaf flutters
to forest floor. Nowhere is
Death more beautiful.

4

First Storm

WINTER'S FIRST SNOWSTORM arrives under cover of night, riding on the shoulders of a boisterous arctic wind. Flake by perfect flake, the wet white sleets down, piling up until, by morning, the younger, more flexible aspens visible from our cabin windows are bowed tip-to-ground, like so many horseshoes turned open-ends down, their luck running out.

When a foot has accumulated, a few aging, ailing quakies, their resolve weakened in the face of yet another long mountain winter, release their existential rooting and make slow, sad pratfalls to stasis. At a snow depth of two feet, more aspens—middle-aged, healthy looking, roots firmly rooted but torsos gone rigid with arthritic disposition—try to resist the indomitable force of mass-times-gravity, are inevitably overwhelmed, snap clean in two and their tops come crashing down; I hear the rifle-sharp cracks of these violent decapitations most every time I venture outdoors to melt snow with used coffee.

On the third day of the storm, I wake from a fitful sleep to find a trio of foot-thick aspens fallen—trunks stacked and limbs tangled—hard against the cabin's front door; I have to exit out the back, shovel my way into the tool shed, retrieve the big orange Stihl and chain-saw-massacre a tunnel to the front door.

That noisome task done, I strap on snowshoes and trudge around inspecting the pale corpses of broke-backed trees. In the open wounds of every victim is exposed the punky tissue symptomatic of heartrot. A discreet and efficient predator is winter's first storm, culling the feeble, the inflexible, the irresolute—a sharp-fanged wolf at work amongst a placid flock.

It's a seeming sylvan disaster now. But come spring, the survivors will emerge leaner, stronger—straightening, stretching, flexing, reaching for the sun, and with more room to grow and prosper—the vigorous products of adversity endured.

Aspen as exemplar.

5

Winter

FEBRUARY.

Ten long weeks have passed since the annual Thanksgiving snow-storm blew in to bury the steep, winding dirt roads that skein across this Colorado mountainside I call home. Although it may sound foreboding, this is good for Caroline and me: As the serious snows arrive each year, so depart the last summer-home vacation residents, packing hurriedly, tacking sheets of plywood over the windows of their prefab cabins, scurrying down and out of the mountains and south to Sun City and similar winter havens.

They leave behind them tranquillity, snow-closed road, and a thankful handful of year-round residents. Admittedly selfish about my solitude (it's so very hard to come by these days), no one is more thankful than I to see them go. That most are good people, good neighbors, matters not one whit. That isn't the point.

A meek sun rides low along the southern sky these brief winter days—that is, when it isn't obscured entirely by the ghostly fog of a whiteout. In such conditions—white above, white below, white all around—the barren aspens picketing our little handmade cabin seem gray, sad, pensive. Or perhaps I'm investing them with my own melancholy.

February, the briefest of months, but sometimes hardly brief enough. The "winter wonderland" of Christmas celebration, at first welcome, when given a few weeks to slip into retrospect loses much of its charm, becomes a drudge. Golden autumn is a mere faint memory, verdant spring a distant dream. Cabin fever is endemic. Put another log on the fire, boil us up another pot of tea. Or better yet, some good strong coffee brewed from stout, exotic beans grown someplace far to the south, a place where brightly colored birds sing for joy in fertile forests and February is the perfect month.

But even here in the frozen white Rockies, even in February, life goes on. Especially around the slender aspen tree where the bird feeder hangs. To this winter oasis come not just birds, but the big, tassel-eared Abert's squirrel; the occasional lean brown cottontail or plump white snowshoe hare, and, keeping watch with winter-hungry eyes from aeries atop nearby spruce, fir or ponderosa, hawks, owls, falcons.

One crackling-cold morning not long ago, as I stood at the kitchen window sipping coffee and watching a mob of Steller's jays fussing over seed, a fleet dark shadow dropped from above to knock one of the dove-sized jays from the feeder perch, pinning it to the ground below.

Accipiter cooperii, Cooper's hawk.

To the hapless jay, alas, the name of its death angel hardly mattered. The hungry hunter settled over its kill, wings shrouded like some feathered Dracula, mantling its prize from any competing carnivore that might be soaring or lurking nearby. The predator fed nervously for a minute or two, plucking hooked beakfuls of sky-blue feathers from the jay's steaming breast, tearing at the warm flesh beneath, pausing frequently to peer around. Then, suddenly and for no reason apparent to me, the hawk took flight with its tattered prize in tow.

It's hard, but it works. Violent death by predation is a disturbingly beautiful event to behold. It's not an image that soon leaves your mind—nor should it, for it carries implications worth personalizing, expanding, pondering.

But life goes on. Just over the hill, half a mile east, big bathtub-shaped depressions melted into the snow show where the hardy handful of elk who winter on this mountain have bedded, the cows among them bearing new life within. New life, wild life—like the rest of us up here, eagerly awaiting the renewal of spring.

Meanwhile, down in the silent world beneath the deep, insulating snow, pocket gophers go about their subterranean business as usual, pushing up furrows of homogenized earth that will collapse into drunken trenchlines with the spring snowmelt. Our half-tame Colorado chipmunks and golden-mantled ground squirrels are snoring the winter away snug in the grass-lined bowls of their earthen dens, rousing from time to time to enjoy their caches of handout sunflower seed and varous wild fare. For the chippers, winter snacking is a handy task, since they use their food stores for mattresses.

Other rodents, wanting to be in or beneath the cabin where it's warm, can be especially pesky in winter. Used to be, Caroline and I endured the company of curious, bug-eyed deer mice (*Peromyscus leucopus*, also known as the white-footed mouse). But since becoming infamous as carriers of the dread hantavirus, they've been forcefully evicted. And when a docile striped skunk tried to move in beneath the cabin, I gently discouraged her by illuminating the crawl space with a forty-watt bulb. To a skunk, if it isn't dark in the daytime, it doesn't feel like home.

Most recently—just weeks ago in fact—Caroline was outside with the dogs, watching the endless snow fall, when she heard "an unfamiliar chittering call, like no bird I've ever heard." She looked that way, but at first saw nothing. Then, from out of the woodpile, burst what she described as "a whirling ball of white." What it was, was an ermine—a winter-white long-tailed weasel—with its barracuda teeth fastened in a death grip to a cottontail's neck ... "our" cottontail, which had been living in the woodpile all winter, emerging every night to nose around for spilt seed beneath the bird feeder.

Otis, our lab-retriever, saw all of this too and in a flash was on the move. Ninety pounds of growling black fury hurtling down on you isn't something easily overlooked, even in the midst of a life-or-death struggle; the ermine released her grip on the bunny and the rabbit streaked away. The ermine took off after the rabbit, Caroline called Otis back. And that was that.

So it goes, high in the Rockies, deep in winter.

∾

Sometimes, on the drabbest of days after a long gray spell, melancholy envelops me like a fog. I lost two well-loved companions recently, one a man, the other man's best friend. Both are too much on my mind as I sit here now on this cold winter's eve, scribbling.

Winter's a long time going, up this high.

I rise from my old oak rocker, step into the big rubber snow boots waiting always by the door, and venture out into the frozen night. All around me the aspens stand tall and straight against the dark and cold, black-eyed ivory pillars glowing eerily under a lean February moon. Already, I'm noticing, the aspen buds are swelling, reddening, blushing with the promise of new life ... come spring.

PART TWO

❧

Natural Histories
and Polemics

6

The Last Grizzly Slayer

THE LAST GRIZZLY SLAYER—the only living former federal trapper to have legally killed a grizzly bear in Colorado—takes up his hand-hewn staff and leads out briskly. We lope past the Weminuche Wilderness boundary sign and start up the long switchback trail toward the Continental Divide and, beyond, Starvation Gulch—so named by old-time miners who prospected there, found nothing and financially "starved out."

After a quarter mile, my guide suddenly stops, like a man who's just remembered he's forgotten something. "Dave," he says, "maybe you should take the lead. I might set too fast a pace."

I smile and step obediently to the front. After all, I'm well into my forties, while my guide, who fears he might leave me in the dust, is barely sixty-nine.

∞

I first heard about Ernest Wilkinson—who he is and what he's done and the fact that he's still kicking—from my friend John Murray's powerful work *Wildlife in Peril*. But I didn't meet the man until this past June, when I drove 125 miles to his taxidermy shop on the outskirts of Monte Vista.

Ernest's Taxidermy: The walls and floors, the parallel rows of shelves, every cranny and nook of the place is home to the indigenous living dead—lifelike mounts of just about every species of wildlife that has ever walked, flown or finned through the southern Rockies.

31

I worked my way to the back of the store, where a worn wooden counter is anchored at one end by an ancient manual cash register. Behind the counter, in an open doorway leading back into what I took to be the workshop, stood an attractive older woman with long silver hair pulled back in thick braids. She introduced herself as Meg. We talked for a while, and I learned that she and Ernie have been together for more than forty years. Like her husband, Margaret Wilkinson has lived her entire life in the spectacular San Luis Valley of south-central Colorado.

After we'd gotten to know each other a bit, Meg waved me back into her husband's cluttered quarters and returned to her work—she fashions leather garments and beadwork so fine that Indians come to *her* for costumes and instruction in these traditional crafts.

Apparently oblivious to my arrival, Ernest Wilkinson sat on a backless stool, his flat stomach pressed against a splintered workbench on which rested the in-progress head mount of a five-point bull elk.

As I glanced about at the furry clutter of backlog crowding the workshop, it struck me that Ernest's taxidermy skills were in high demand. "Either you do good work," I ventured as an opener, "or your prices are right."

Wilkinson looked up. "Both," he said, fighting a smile.

As soon as he'd tied off the stitch he was lacing, Wilkinson extended a leathery hand with deeply split brown nails—a hand, I mused as we shook, that had been stained by the blood of three Colorado grizzlies: his own 1951 Starvation Gulch bear, the Blue Lake boar killed a month earlier, and the '79 Wiseman grizzly, the purported "last grizzly in Colorado," whose gorgeous pelt Wilkinson had prepared for the Denver Museum of Natural History.

Ernie is not a large man—five-nine maybe, 150 pounds perhaps, but possessed of a mesomorphic youthfulness that belies his seven decades. His face is round and friendly, the smiling eyes overshadowed by heavy brows, the skin tan and not nearly so wrinkled as the corrugated mountains in which he's spent his life. Quiet, unaffected and instantly likable.

Ernie dragged up a rickety wooden chair for me, I hauled out my cheap tape recorder and we launched into the interview I'd come for. As we talked, my host continued his work.

Born in 1924 on a ranch near Monte Vista, Wilkinson grew up hunting and fishing and trapping. When he came out of the army following World War II, he hired on as a government trapper with PARC, the Department of Interior's bureau of Predator and Rodent Control, "taking care of coyotes and bears where they were doing damage to livestock."

It was work he could do, in country he knew and loved. And back then, when the Rocky Mountain West was still something of a frontier, killing predators that preyed on livestock was considered necessary and honorable work. There was a job to be done, and here was a man to do it.

During the nine years he worked as a federal trapper—seven full-time, two part-time—Wilkinson killed hundreds of coyotes but "not too many" bears. I asked how many was not too many.

"Twenty-six, twenty-seven maybe. Not too many."

Notwithstanding his skill and effectiveness as a predator killer, Ernie lacked the patriotic dedication to his work shared by most federal trappers, and was openly critical of at least a couple of PARC's policies.

"Most government trappers," he complained, "were big on using poisons. They'd dope animal carcasses, and in winter scatter strychnine-soaked tallow balls from horseback or drop 'em by the paper bagfuls from airplanes wherever sheep and cattle were going to be grazed come spring. Any animal or bird that ate one of those baits— coyote, bear, lion, eagle, raven, pine martin, ranch dog, you name it—died. And whatever scavengers that came along to feed on the corpses of the poison victims, they died too. I never went for that. Too indiscriminate."

Wilkinson's disenchantment with PARC's "toxic Johnny Apple-seed" techniques and body-count mentality, together with his marriage in 1952 to Margaret, prompted him to take an early semiretirement, becoming a weekends-only government trapper. "Even then," he quietly boasted, "I usually caught more problem bears than most guys who worked full-time; I knew the country so much better than anyone else."

After a couple more years, Wilkinson quit PARC for good, preferring to stay home with Meg and nurse his infant taxidermy business. By then, the Wilkinsons had built the house and shop they occupy yet today.

Times were hard back then, so in the winters Ernie ran a trapline for furs and food—the Wilkinsons are masters of economizing and will eat almost anything edible, including bobcat. To rake in a few extra dimes during the summer tourist season, they built a small zoo adjacent to the shop and filled it with indigenous wildlife. Ernie soon discovered he had a talent for training wild animals and before long was providing four-footed actors—black bears, cougars, badgers, bobcats—for movies and television.

"If you've seen John Wayne's *Chisholm Trail*," Ernie told me, "or the TV shows *Wild Kingdom, Wild World of Animals,* or *American Sportsman,* you've seen my animals."

With such compliant models at hand, it was only natural that Ernie should get into wildlife photography as well.

Today, the little zoo is empty, grown up in weeds, and wears a weathered "Closed" sign. Ernie's actors all grew old and died, and he never bothered to replace them; too much time required for the training, he explained.

Wilkinson can't recall exactly when he began writing, but since 1968 his locally syndicated "Outdoor Tips and Tales" column has appeared in area newspapers. He has published articles in national outdoor magazines, authored a long-selling book called *Snow Caves for Fun and Survival* and in his "spare time" has completed the first 151 pages of the autobiography of a modern-day mountain man.

Additionally and amazingly, the old mountaineer, together with a younger partner, runs a school called Trail Skills, Inc., through which Ernie teaches survival and primitive skills workshops and leads wilderness backpack treks. This summer, he says, is typical, with four week-long hiking expeditions scheduled back-to-back. The first involves guiding a group of "senior citizens" (his term) through some of the loftiest and most spectacular of Rio Grande backcountry.

The years, as they say, have been kind to Wilkinson. Until trapping was banned (by popular vote) in Colorado in 1996, his winter trap-lines got no shorter, covering up to twenty miles through terrain so physically challenging that most hikers eschew it even in summer. The old adventurer crammed everything into a big backpack and cross-country skied when possible, snowshoed when necessary. Never carried a tent, preferring to bivouac under a tree or dig a snow cave.

Our conversation turned to bears.

Back in the summer of 1951, his twenty-seventh year, Ernie was responsible for predator control for fifty-three sheep camps scattered from the headwaters of the Rio Grande east all the way to Creede and south as far as Wagon Wheel Gap. His base camp that season was at Brewster Park, a broad willow-flat along the river.

Over the years, Ernie had come to know the names and personalities of all of his client shepherds—young Mexicans, Basques and Indians. "Herding sheep in the mountains is lonely work," he'll tell you. "The herders would always welcome me into their camps in a big way, offering coffee and their favorite treat, canned jam on camp-made bread. It's an experience a lot of people will never have," he reflected, monumentally understating, "riding every day, learning every wrinkle of the land, camping alone every night, living out of a pack-saddle."

Ernie's patrol circuits were anywhere from three to thirteen days long, then he'd return to Brewster Park to replenish his supplies and check his "complaint list"—in his absence, Forest Service rangers or sheep ranchers or herders would sometimes drop by and leave notes telling him where they were having predator trouble. When that happened, he'd "pack up some grub and ride right back out again."

I asked if he had practiced the so-called preventive control so popular with federal trappers then and now—killing predators before they cause trouble, presuming sooner or later they will.

"I worked on coyotes all the time," he said. "But I took bears only when they acted up. Many's the time while out riding, I'd see a bear; he'd be right there, and I could easy have pulled out the 250/3000 Savage rifle I carried in my saddle scabbard and shot him. But I didn't. And sometimes on a deal like that, it wouldn't be but a week and I'd have to go back in there because that same bear had turned to killing sheep. Other times, bears would hang around a camp all summer and not bother a thing. Some trappers would kill every bear they came across, whether it was causing trouble or not; there was a lot of pressure on us for numbers. But I couldn't see it. Just like the poisoning—I didn't like it, and I didn't do it."

I asked about the grizzly.

"I got word they were having trouble up at Starvation Gulch; a bear had gotten into a herd of a thousand or so sheep a rancher named Hutchinson was grazing there; it's a pretty big place, once you get in there. The day before I arrived, the herder had moved the flock up out of the gulch, away from where the bear had come out of the trees during the night to kill several sheep. But there were carcasses still lying around, only partially eaten, and I knew the bear would come back to work on them some more. So that's where I set up to get him."

That done, Wilkinson rode south over Hunchback Pass, around Ute Mountain and down into Ute Creek—a day each way plus working time—"to take care of some coyote problems." Before pulling out, he asked the Mexican herder—Amarante Roybal is the name he recalls—"to go down into the gulch every day and check to see if the bear had come back."

When Ernie returned to Starvation three days later, on September 5, he asked Roybal if he'd seen the bear. "Oh no," said the herder, whose halting English Ernie dramatically recreated for me. "Me no go down there alone. It *dark* down there."

"Amarante, like most herders, was scared to death of bears," Ernie explained. "So I rode on down off the ridge and into the gulch, and there was the bear, dead, rolled over on his back with his legs sticking up in the air. The days had been warm, and he was already bloated."

It was a male, two or three years old, 250 or 275 pounds, and heavily muscled. The pelt was in fall prime, colored dark brown with yellow and silvery guard hairs. The taxidermist in Ernie thought it would have made a beautiful rug, but flies had already blown (deposited eggs in) the flesh, the hair was slipping and the corpse stank too much to mess with. Only the right front paw, sticking up in the air away from the putrescent carcass, remained unspoiled. Noticing the extraordinarily long claws, Ernie cut off the paw, fleshed it out and rubbed it down with salt to preserve it. He still has it today, trotting it out to show students in his wilderness skills classes the difference between black bear and grizzly tracks.

At this juncture, Wilkinson led me out into the storefront, fished around in a huge cardboard boxful of furry bits and produced the paw for my inspection. The gray palm and toe pads, though rough like a dog's, were still pliable after forty-two years. The palm pad measured three inches front to back and four inches across. Taken together, the toes were slightly wider than the palm, fused at their bases and arranged in a nearly straight line—not separated by hair and steeply arced like a black bear's. The claws were yellowish and slightly curved, with the longest measuring almost three inches. The claw tips were only modestly worn, suggesting that the young bear had not been doing a lot of digging, had not yet prepared his winter's den.

When I asked how he'd gone about trapping the animal, Ernie thought a long while before answering.

"Well, you generally want to build a triangular log pen, or cubby, near the trail the bear has been using. If you get up on a high point right at daybreak, you can see where the bear has walked through the grass the night before and knocked the dew off. So you build your cubby near the trail and drag a sheep carcass over and stuff it into the point at the back of the triangle. Then you conceal your trap at the entrance so that the bear will have to step into it when he goes for the bait. That way, you're fairly sure of getting the right bear, the one that's been causing the trouble; they usually come back to clean up their leftovers."

What kind of trap had he used?

"In bear traps, I like either a No. 5 or a No. 15 Victor, the only difference between the two being that one has teeth and the other doesn't. Rumors say I used a No. 6 Newhouse to catch that grizzly, but I didn't. Those things were too big and heavy to haul around, even on horseback; weighed more than forty pounds. Besides, I didn't know it was a grizzly that had been into the sheep; just naturally assumed it was a black bear. And the No. 5 is plenty big enough for black bear. Just chain it to a tree so's your bear can't drag it off."

Did he know it was a grizzly as soon as he saw it?

"No. It just struck me as a big bear with pretty fur and long claws. There was a lightning storm, and all I was thinking about was taking care of things as quick as possible and getting down out of there before I got fried. So I didn't pay too much attention. I just cut off that one paw and scalped the ears—which we were required to bring in to verify our kills—to take to my boss, district supervisor Lee Bacus down in Monte Vista."

When young Ernie showed Bacus the scalp and paw, the senior PARC man immediately recognized the long claws and light guard hairs as grizzly. "Lee asked about the skull," Ernie recalled. "He wanted to know if I'd brought it out. I told him no, that the corpse was stinking and a storm was on and I hadn't even thought about it. But I was headed back up there in a couple of weeks to go elk hunting, so I offered to pick it up then."

Ernie tried to make good on that offer, but scavengers had picked the carcass clean and broken and scattered the bones like shells on a beach. The skull was nowhere to be found.

"Wish I could have located it," Ernie reflected. "It would be worth something today, with grizzlies so rare and all."

Had he ever given any thought to the possibility of grizzlies being around before the Starvation bear turned up? Had there been any gossip—local people with stories about seeing grizzlies or grizzly sign?

"No on both counts," said Ernie, explaining that back then, there *were* no local people living up that high. "Just a few sheepherders in summer, and most of them didn't speak English."

When word got out about the Starvation grizzly, the Colorado Division of Wildlife "got all excited," promptly designating the upper Rio Grande as a grizzly bear management area and making it illegal to kill the great bears there. Not long after, laws were passed protecting the grizzly statewide. At least on paper. If any could still be found to protect.

"As part of the deal," Ernie chuckled, "the Division sent a man up to look around for more grizzlies. He spent two summers up there but didn't find a thing so far as I know. Spent a lot of time down here at the shop too, studying the differences between grizzly and black bear hair and paws, trying to figure it out as he went along."

At this point, I turned the conversation to the Blue Lake grizzly, from whose spoiled hide Wilkinson had salvaged the head mount still on display at the Skyline Lodge in the tiny tourist town of Platoro, along the Conejos River in the South San Juans.

"Like my own bear," he said, "it was a male, big compared to most blackies but small for a grizzly. In fact, I've always suspected that the two were twins. They were both the same age, about two and a half, same size, same color, right down the line. They could have been just recently turned out by their mother, which would help explain why they both got into trouble with sheep at about the same time."

Entirely plausible. It's subadult males of all species, predators in particular, who do the most wandering and lurching about, and thus, who fall into the most trouble (I recall my own rocky youth). They've been pushed out of their childhood territories, either by a mother ready to breed again or by a mature male that sees them as competition, and have to go in search of a new home. They're inexperienced and, consequently, often hungry and desperate.

"A young bear like that could cover the distance between Starvation Gulch and Blue Lake in a couple of days or less," my host suggested.

As tactfully as I could manage, I next asked Ernie how he feels today about having killed one of the dead-last grizzlies in Colorado.

"Can't say I'm proud of it. But if a predator was killing sheep, it was my job to take care of him."

"Yes," I agreed, "it was your job, and grizzlies weren't protected then, and it was unintentional to boot—you had no reason to suspect it would be a grizzly. But still, what are your feelings about it now, since grizzlies have been almost entirely wiped out in the lower forty-eight? Would you change anything if you knew it was a grizzly and had it to do again?"

"Well … I could have done a better job of documenting the circumstances of the kill. And I wish I'd taken pictures."

I gave up. The retrospective remorse I was probing for just wasn't there. Ernest Wilkinson simply does not view any aspect of his grizzly slaying as deserving of guilt. It was his job. It was unintentional. It was legal. It was just something that happened. I didn't argue. There was nothing to argue about.

I had not come to Ernest's Taxidermy expecting to make a new friend. My intent was simply to get the story of the Starvation grizzly's death, then leave. But after talking with Ernie for a few hours and getting to know him and finding myself enjoying his company, I suggested that we hike into Starvation together. I wanted to see the place, and I'd need a guide to find the exact spot. Ernie allowed as how he wouldn't mind visiting Starvation again. It had, after all, been forty-two years.

❧

Peaking at a relatively measly 10,833 feet above sea level, Timber Hill is more or less the midpoint, though far short of the high point, between the old San Juan mining towns of Silverton to the northwest and Creede to the east. In accordance with the plan we'd hatched back in June at his shop, Ernie and I rendezvoused at the Lost Trail Ranch above Rio Grande Reservoir, where he conducts his Wilderness Skills classes. We left his old pumpkin-colored van parked under a shade tree there and bumped the last spine-shattering miles up to Timber Hill in my old four-by-four.

I can't imagine enduring Stony Pass in a tipsy stagecoach or on the hard plank seat of an ore wagon, which the rocky old roadway was built to accommodate over a century ago, with precious few improvements since. In several places, talus slides and deep stream crossings make it nearly impassable, even for my high-slung pickup.

By the time we arrived at camp, only a couple of hours of light remained and electric-blue storm clouds threatened; July is the most pyrotechnic of months in the southern Rockies. We set about dragging in an evening's supply of firewood, from which Ernie selected several match-sized sticks of "squaw wood" and deftly arranged a tepee in the center of some previous roadside campers' fire ring. Beneath this he inserted a splintery "fuzz stick" whittled on the spot, and struck a one-match blaze.

As the flames grew, Ernie produced a "billy can"—a gallon vegetable tin—filled it with creek water and dropped in the dinners he had generously volunteered to provide: military-issue "meals ready to eat" in foil bags. After these feasts had simmered for five minutes, chef Ernie fished them out and asked if I wanted a cup of coffee, nodding at the boiling billy water.

I studied the greenish scum floating on top and hesitated.

My companion shrugged. "That's just the ink that boiled off the food pouches. Don't taste so bad. I drink it all the time."

By way of compromise, I filtered a cupful of the glaucous liquid through a paper towel and added a double spoonful of instant caffeine.

Over dinner, Ernie explained his plan of attack for the morning: We would leave my truck there at Timber Hill and scramble down into the canyon of the Rio Grande, carrying fly rods and waders in addition to lunches and rain gear (and for me, tape recorder and camera). At the river, we would don the waders and ford the icy water, cache waders and fishing gear on the far bank and claw our way up through the near-vertical terrain, cliff upon cliff, and into the dark timber above. There we could "probably" pick up an elk trail leading into the bottom of the gulch. Then it would be a final hump of a mile or so up through the belly of the beast to its head, near where the now-mythical grizzly deed had been done.

When I surveyed Starvation Gulch with the naked eye from our camp—looking out across the six-hundred-foot ditch of the Rio Grande and up endless rows of stepped cliffs and through a mile or more of spruce-fir forest as thick and black as a new-moon midnight (and sure to be stacked neck-high in blowdown)—the place seemed as foreign and foreboding as Detroit.

On a topographical map, it's only about three miles straight-line from the head of the gulch down to the river. On the ground, however, there are no straight lines, the rugged terrain effectively doubling the distance and turning the whole thing into God's own obstacle course. Naked alpine peaks, most of them rising above thirteen thousand feet, guard the gulch on three sides, with the forest and river canyon forming a challenging barrier against approach from below. The spot Ernie had marked on the map as our goal—about where he figures he'd bagged the bear—waited at 11,400 feet. Viewed from Timber Hill, it seemed all too obvious why Starvation Gulch had been among the last grizzly holdouts in the entire Southwest.

I reacted to this maniacally ambitious plan with a groan. Considering distance, altitude gain and nastiness of topography going up, then allowing who knows how much time to poke around trying to find the exact spot where Ernie had slain the bear—eat lunch, talk, take pictures—then the steep scramble back down, fording the river and grunting out of the canyon back up to camp (with quite likely an afternoon lightning and hail storm tossed in for spice), not to mention Ernie's desire to do some evening fly fishing down in the canyon ... to attempt all of that in the space of just one brief day, I tactfully suggested, might be pushing things just a wee bit, even by Wilkinson's hiker-from-hell standards.

Still, I was resigned to giving it a go, but only if there was no easier way. As an afterthought, I asked Ernie how folks managed to get sheep in and out of there, and how he'd done it on horseback.

"Oh," he said, "there's other ways in. I suppose we could drive up to Beartown at first light—assuming the road didn't wash out during the spring melt-off—hike east over the Divide, and drop down into Starvation from the top. Trouble with that route is that we'd have to climb back over the Divide to get out. You might be tired by then."

Indeed I might.

"And if we go in that way, we won't get to fish."

Shucks.

With dinner finished and our greenish swill swallowed, we admired the last violet streaks of an alpine sunset fading beyond the jagged horizon as heat lightning strobed in the distance. Ernie allowed as how it would probably be a good idea to go ahead and make up our beds, in case a sudden storm should come up. "Tag along," suggested the old woodsman, grinning that shy sly grin of his. "You might learn something."

Dragging an eight-foot aspen pole behind him—I'd wondered why he wouldn't let me break it up for firewood—Ernie wandered around for a minute before selecting an open spot beneath a fat, low-limbed spruce. "Time me," he said.

I glanced at my watch—9:18 P.M. Getting dark.

Without appearing to rush, Ernie positioned the aspen limb on
the ground parallel to the slope and about three feet out from the
spruce, anchoring it in place with several fist-sized rocks wedged in
below. Then, dropping to his knees, he began raking up the spruce
needles that littered the ground beneath and around the tree, tossing
them into the cavity formed between the trunk above and the
aspen-limb dam below.

As he worked, Ernie explained that the thick cushion of needles he
was piling up would level the slope, make a soft mattress, provide
insulation from the chilly ground and, should it rain, allow water to
flow beneath, keeping his bed high and dry. Finally, he spread his
nylon rain poncho over the needle mattress, unrolled a small sleeping bag encased in a waterproof Gore-Tex bivy sack Meg had sewn
up for him and … "How long?"

I checked—9:22. "Four minutes. Flat."

My turn. I walked over to my pickup, unrolled and blew up my
"self-inflating" sleeping pad, unrolled and spread out my sleep sack.
I'd just made a one-minute berth in the tin-covered bed of my truck
… but somehow the victory was hollow.

A leak was taken, a splash of whiskey was poured (Ernie declined),
the fire was stirred and fed wood enough to last another hour or so,
and quiet conversation ensued until sack time. Up the black mountain somewhere to the west, a bull elk wailed out one tentative bugle.
July 24: a full month earlier than I'd ever heard that magical autumn
sound before.

ॐ

Overnight, the clouds moved through without dropping their
dreaded rain. The morning is clear and cool, ideal for a vigorous hike
into the unknown territory of natural and unnatural history.
Walking in the lead now, I take it easy, in no particular hurry, conserving my energies—though for what, I can't yet say. That's why I'm
conserving.

Our daybreak drive from Timber Hill up to Beartown was, well, interesting. We splashed across the Rio Grande near its headwaters, where the flow looked only a foot deep in the flat morning light but proved to be twice that, then low-geared up the Bear Creek "road" to the old Beartown site: 11,162 feet into the sky, a century dead and not so much as a plank left of what was once a booming mining camp and top-of-the-world stage station.

While side-hilling up a particularly steep stretch of trail, I hear, just ahead, the distinctive *chunk … chunk … chunk* that signals mule deer; muleys don't run so much as they pogo, like the stotting of African antelopes. I scan the forest for a glimpse of the fleeing animal but see only trees. Just three big bounds had been enough to conceal the nervous muley behind a bushy wall of Engelmann spruce, subalpine fir and a waist-high understory of forbs and ferns. Had the animal merely stood still as a statue, or ghosted silently away as bears are wont to do, we would probably have walked right past without ever knowing it was there. Forest hikers would be surprised to know how often they pass close by not only deer, but bears, those masters at seeing without being seen, of silent comings and goings.

Grizzly bears are said to be capable of identifying the upwind odor of humans at nearly a mile and can hear normal conversation at more than three hundred yards. These keen senses, combined with their genetic shyness and inclination to flee from humans at speeds up to thirty miles an hour, account for the rarity of grizzly sightings in the wild. Unless, of course, you're hiking in silence into the wind and bump into one at close range. In such instances, while a black bear will almost always either remain hidden until the danger passes or run away, a grizzly is far less predictable. Which, after all, is what makes them grizzlies.

Now the trail dips into the narrow cut of a glassy snowmelt brook. Just yards below where the little stream slides over the trail, its course is dammed by the moss-shrouded corpse of a huge fallen tree. In and around the resultant mini-marsh grow sedges, skunk cabbages and a dazzling profusion of mountain bluebells.

Ernie takes this gorgeous little garden as a cue to launch into an impromptu wilderness skills class, describing which parts of which wild plants are edible and when, and how best to prepare them; warning of the extreme toxicity of the skunk cabbage, more properly called false hellebore or corn lily (*Veratrum californicum,* not to be confused with *Lysichitum americanum,* the innocuous yellow skunk cabbage of the Pacific Northwest and Montana), then informing me that parturient elk cows seek out lush growths of bluebells like this in which to "throw" their June calves and that elk and bears and domestic sheep and cattle all hanker after the tasty pink-blue beauties.

Farther along, Ernie stops and bends down to examine a big dry puffball protruding from the dark mountain soil. "If you've got a bad cut or a bleeding wound of any kind," he says, "find one of these and bust it open"—he pricks the big rust-colored fungus with a quick brown finger and a billion spores rise like smoke—"hold it against the wound; it'll staunch the bleeding and prevent infection."

And so it goes, through a most informative morning's hike.

By and by the switchbacks line out, the old-growth forest falls behind and we enter a narrow strip of krummholz, the eerie pygmy "bent wood" ecology that demarks timberline. The open tundra lies just ahead, just above. When we attain the crest, Ernie stops to survey the scene. A faint path, hardly even a proper game trail, skeins out to our left, weaving through tufts of grass and low-growing alpine wildflowers, tracking north along Indian Ridge. "This way," says my guide, dodging around me.

The hike so far, though vigorous, hasn't been bad. And now that we're on top and hiking off-trail, the way is almost level and almost easy, even at a little better than twelve grand ASL.

We walk for a while and then there it is—the sparkling many-fingered headwaters of Starvation Creek, only a mile or so away and six hundred feet below us. Thanks to Ernie's steel-trap memory and uncanny sense of direction, we have come in blind and wound up exactly where we want to be.

Viewed from above, the ominous Starvation Gulch is revealed as a verdant, gently sloping subalpine park ringed with dark timber and set about by the ten primary peaks of Ute Ridge. This place, gentle and welcoming, bears no resemblance whatsoever to the impenetrable hellhole it seems from Timber Hill. Along its grassy edges, the meadow is penetrated here and there by stubby fingers of conifers— one of which marks the last stand of a now-famous Colorado grizzly.

We angle down toward the cirque and come to a rill of icy water. Ernie kneels at its edge, removes his ancient grime-stiffened felt hat— at sixty-nine, he still has a full head of hair, damn him—dips the hat in, raises it and drinks deep from its flooded brim. Water diamonds drip from his chin as he grins at me. "Beats carrying a canteen."

Now the old trapper stands and points to a small knoll a few hundred yards below, overlooking the head of the gulch. I agree with Ernie's suggestion that it's an ideal aerie from which to inspect the park, and we angle steeply down toward it.

As we walk, we spot a serpentine line of tan dots emerging from the gully of Snowslide Creek, out near the center of the gulch. The animals are taking their sweet old time single-filing toward an avalanche chute sandwiched between two timber stringers directly opposite. We stop and raise our binoculars to confirm the obvious: elk.

Long after we've reached the knoll and plopped down in the cool grass to watch, the elk still come. When the last of the stragglers finally disappears into the timber, we agree that the herd comprised at least eighty of the big deer. Ernie says he's run into batches of two hundred' and more up nearby Pole Creek. No doubt he has, but this is the largest gathering of elk I've ever been blessed to see—discounting Yellowstone Park, and the wapiti by the hundreds that winter, docile as cattle, along the Animas River just north of Durango. (Or used to; most of the best of that former ranch pasture was recently transmogrified into Durango's third golf course, replete with a tacky gaggle of greens-side trophy homes for the pretentious half-rich.)

Directly below us, almost within a rock's toss, stands an island of spindly spruce and fir, bunched together as if for security. Around this oblong of trees wraps a broad marsh grown waist-high in a tangle of subalpine willow. Moose nirvana. In fact, the local game warden asked me to watch for a moose cow and calf that were thought to have wintered up here and haven't been seen since fall. Nor, I'm afraid, are they apparent now.

Instead, we are graced with the sudden appearance of a plump, steel-gray coyote. Either unaware or uncaring that two humans are sitting within easy shooting range of her—for some reason, I take it for a female—the bemused dog tends to its business, nose to the damp ground, sniffing at a fast trot toward the little copse of conifers directly below us and disappearing forthwith therein.

A few minutes later, a second coyote materializes at the willows' edge. This beast, which I take to be the other's mate, is noticeably larger and looks as old and raggedy as I sometimes feel, enjoying perhaps his last golden summer on this heavenly earth. More cautious than his partner, the wise old dog raises his scruffy face, peers up at us, twitches his nose in disdainful recognition, then turns and melts back into the marsh thicket.

All this time, Ernie says nothing. What, I wonder, is he thinking? As a man who's devoted a lifetime to "taking care" of coyotes, is he wishing he had a rifle? Is he judging the value of the pelt? Or can he, like the best of hunters, distance himself from the chase enough to appreciate wild nature for its own sake? Doubting a definitive answer, I don't even ask.

After a while, having picked out our route, we ease down the abrupt slope into the head of the gulch, skirting the sprawling sedge and willow marsh as best we can.

The sun falls warm on our faces, and the cool air carries the mixed perfume of wildflowers: ubiquitous dandelions, bashful little striped geraniums, alpine bistort like cotton balls on sticks, purple monkshoods and fringed gentians and sticky asters, plus a fortune in anonymous others scattered like living jewels across the park. Along the soggy marsh edges and frequent snowmelt trickles grow lavender shooting stars, big white-trimmed blue columbines (Colorado's state flower), delicate cushions of pink moss campion, white-flowered watercress by the bushel.

We reach the far edge of the cirque and halt to hatch a strategy. Ernie allows as how he'll walk in the open a few yards out from the trees, looking for familiar scenery and bleached bits of bone he hopes may still be lying about even after so very long. I propose to keep just inside the undulant tree line, looking for the log remains of the cubby, which I suspect are more likely than bone to have survived four decades of brutal alpine winters. Ernie shrugs, as if to say he considers this ploy a waste of time, but says nothing. We start slowly down the park.

The quarry proves elusive. No bone, no rotting V of logs, no nothing except heart-cracking scenery, the cleanest air and water in the world and, lurking in my head, a mildly troubling confusion of feelings about being here.

After half an hour of snooping down the park edge, four probing eyes glued to the ground, Ernie announces lunchtime. I follow him out to a glacial erratic, a Volkswagen-sized boulder stranded a hundred yards out in the meadow, onto whose sun-warmed, lichen-stained antiquity we climb. Perched thus, like a couple of overstuffed marmots, we unpack our brown bags and eat.

Offering the ingenuous smile that by now I've learned indicates a modest self-embarrassment, Ernie takes me entirely off-guard by suddenly announcing, "There's no point in you searching for a cubby, because there ain't one here; never was."

"But I thought you said you built a pen and stuffed a dead sheep in and set a trap, and that's how you took the grizzly."

"Never said any such. That was the assumption you came in with; probably read it somewhere. I just let you keep believing that way, just like I've let everybody else believe all these years. I'm telling you now, though, that it didn't happen like that. I've always worried that if some do-good journalist ever got hold of the truth, he'd twist it around and make it sound worse than it was. But I know that this Colorado grizzly thing, getting the story right, is important to you, so I'm going to tell you something I've never told anybody else but Meg … I didn't trap that grizzly."

Ernest Wilkinson looks off toward the trees, seeing things I never will.

"I killed it with a coyote-getter—a cyanide set gun. There was no law back then against using them on national forest lands, and I didn't have much other choice. I only had one trap left by the time I got up here, and the way it worked out I needed two."

Ernie falls into quiet reflection, and I recall how, when I'd interviewed him at his shop and asked if he'd used a cubby and what kind of trap it had been, he'd hesitated, then dropped into a second-person narrative of how catching a bear was usually done, and how he generally preferred the No. 5 Victor—but he never actually said he'd used a cubby or a leg hold trap here in Starvation. Nor, of course, had he denied it. The sly old fox.

But now Ernie owns up, explaining that by the time he got up here, the herder had moved his sheep across the park and up onto the flank of Indian Ridge, trying to get away from the marauding bear. To ease the herder's fears, Ernie placed his last steel trap over there amongst the sheep.

To cover the high-odds return-for-the-leftovers angle, Ernie set out the only other weapon he had left in his depleted arsenal, the coyote-getter. He found a sheep carcass that had plenty of smelly meat still on, hitched it to his horse and dragged it over to where the bear's trail emerged from the trees. That done, he placed the little cyanide gun next to the ripe bait and coated its cotton bait-ball trigger with honey.

"In order to use a second bear trap," Ernie explains now, "it would have meant most of a day's ride down to the Rio Grande where my vehicle was parked, then a ninety-mile round-trip to the warehouse in Monte Vista for another trap, then back up here. A few weeks before, a black bear had killed thirty-four sheep in one night before I got him, and I figured the best way to avoid another such carnage was to use the coyote-getter baited with a dab of honey from my grub sack.

"That bear was dead within seconds of biting the bait," Ernie assures me. "Didn't make it but a few yards before he went down. Probably happened the first night. That's why he was already bloated and stinking by the time I got back here three days later. If he'd been caught in a leg-hold trap, he'd probably have stayed alive and suffered all that time. There was nothing illegal about it, nothing cruel. A blast of cyanide down the throat's the fastest and most humane way I know to kill an animal. Still, I've always worried about admitting it; I'm trusting you to tell it right."

I promise to do my best. Ernie nods, looks away, slices open a grapefruit.

From somewhere back in the woods erupts a chorus of birdlike chirps—elk cows talking with their calves. They've heard us, or smelled us, probably both, but apparently don't feel sufficiently threatened to stampede away. A shadow slides along the ground in front of us. I glance up and see a pair of what I make to be prairie falcons, hanging against the azure vastness like Japanese kites. They circle twice, then sail away, sliding smoothly down the upslope breeze.

We stash our lunch trash in our packs and resume our hunt.

Ernie has decided that the place we're looking for must be near the avalanche chute where the elk disappeared this morning, just below us now. We stroll on down, and it takes only seconds for my guide to pronounce that this is in fact *the place*. He knows for sure, he says, because here's the hulk of an old salt log—a foot-thick log maybe fifteen feet long with a channel axed along the full length of its top, creating a shallow trough into which young Amarante Roybal would have poured rock salt to encourage his sheep to stay in the area, much as compressed salt blocks are used by stockmen today to encourage their hooved hordes to overgraze delicate riparian areas on public land.

We're standing now just below the tip of a stringer of evergreens extending a few yards out into the park, the little trees paralleling a shallow drainage running down from the avalanche chute. Following the chute up into the woods is a deeply incised game trail freshly pocked with the tracks of many elk; their funky smell lingers in the air like the scent of a woman. Major game runways such as this can be centuries old, and I reflect sadly that it could be the selfsame path a certain young grizzly followed to extinction on or about September 3, 1951.

We mill around *the place* for an hour or so, looking for bone fragments but finding none, taking pictures, talking little, thinking each his own thoughts.

We are not always of like mind, Ernie and I. He is of the old-line western rural school that enthusiastically endorses "multiple use" of public lands—grazing in particular—and resents the intervention of "metropolitan people who have messed up their own environments and now are attempting to tell us country folks how to manage our public lands, which mostly are still in good shape."

My own eyes and experiences run contrary, having led me to believe that too many years of too little regulation have led too many western ranchers to view public lands as exclusively theirs, and, together with sympathetic federal land managers, to interpret "multiple use" to mean commodities production above maintaining a healthy and natural ecology.

Former U.S. Forest Service chief Jack Ward Thomas (a biologist rather than a forester by training and experience) summed up the philosophical dichotomy separating Ernie and me: "Some tend to be anthropocentric and take a utilitarian view of land—that is, land exists for people and is to be managed to satisfy people's needs. Others are mainly biocentric in their philosophy, view humans as part of nature and are concerned with organic wholeness."

Ernie is clearly in the former camp; I'm rooted in the latter. Even so, I like and respect Mr. Wilkinson and believe him big enough to grant equal tolerance to me. "Honest men," as an old friend once counseled, "have a right to disagree."

"I just remembered something else," Ernie says as we're preparing to leave.

"When I came back up here elk hunting a couple of weeks after I'd taken the bear—that time when I looked for the skull and couldn't find it—I was riding down off Hunchback Pass there," he points, "and spotted some huge tracks crossing a patch of snow. Biggest bear tracks I've ever seen. One that was still fairly clear was maybe a foot long by half a foot wide, but a little melted out from the sun, so that no claw marks showed. I remember wondering if it might not have been a big old sow grizzly coming down through here, the mother of the young male I'd killed, looking for him. And maybe the mother of that look-alike Blue Lake grizzly as well. Who knows? It was a really big track. Of course, that was a real long time ago."

That it was.

The day is running out, and after a while, though neither of us really wishes to, we turn our backs on this pristine killing field, the last grizzly slayer and me, and silently walk away.

7

What the Animals Know

I'M DAY-HIKING THROUGH a wildly beautiful Colorado mountain meadow, several miles from my camp and a thousand feet below the Continental Divide, when the sky suddenly goes dark. My day adrift in nature, I fear, is about to hit the fan.

Sure enough, within minutes I'm under assault by lightning, thunder, rain like a car wash and swirling fog—your standard surprise September storm here in the high San Juans. And par for my course, my high-dollar, high-tech rain suit is back in camp (where it won't get wet). When hail like shrapnel joins the attack I flee like some panicked animal for the iffy shelter of the nearest finger of forest.

As I enter the dripping woods, something huge and vaguely ominous materializes just ahead, then fades into the gloom. This is dead-center the only place in Colorado that might still hide a final few ghostly grizzlies, and my pulse quickens at the possibility. Then comes a brief thudding of hooves.

I hurry over to where the mysterious animal had been bedded and there, at the leeward base of an umbrella-limbed old-growth spruce, I find a big oval of cushy duff scraped clean of ground litter. And dry as Noah's socks. My nose confirms it: wapiti. I gratefully claim the earthy ark for my own and settle in for the duration of the storm.

Amazing, the elk's ability to locate such efficacious refuge as this, albeit the result of mere mindless instinct, I suppose, like a dog circling before it lies down. An innate inclination hard-wired into the beast's cerebral circuits through countless millennia of selective reinforcement. Or, perhaps, finding nest sites that will remain sheltered and dry in most any weather is a learned skill in elk, passed down from cow to calf, generation to generation. The wapiti aren't saying.

My curiosity stirred by circumstance and with time on my hands, perhaps all night if this storm insists, I'm soon lost in the maze of an old familiar conundrum: What do the animals know?

∾

Certainly, animals know more than we do about comfort, navigation, survival and other such basics of "woodscraftship." Witness the ptarmigan, an alpine grouse that escapes killing blizzards by diving into powdery snow, wherein it finds shelter from screaming arctic winds and insulation against the sub-zero cold. Arctic fox and hares do much the same. Thus did each of these humble beasts independently invent the emergency snow cave.

At the opposite extreme, desert animals know enough to take care of business at night and along the cool edges of twilight, then siesta in shady hidey-holes during the frying hours—thus defeating dehydration, heat prostration, sunburn, cataracts and scorched feet while demonstrating a basic sort of intelligence that's rare, sometimes fatally so, among human desert rats.

And animals know enough to relax and enjoy life. Just the other day a hiking companion and I were sitting quietly in the shade of a tree watching some mallards fool around in a beaver pond a few yards to our front. Suddenly a lone cow elk came bounding out of the woods nearby and leapt explosively into the pond, sending the ducks into panicked flight and little waves sloshing onto the shore. For the next quarter-hour we spied as the big deer splashed, submarined, blew bubbles, kicked the water and stared, mesmerized, at the waves she'd made.

Clearly, this was no example of the "training behavior" so often cited by biologists as the practical motivation for play in young animals. This was a quarter-ton adult. Nor did the elk's aquatic freak-out serve any apparent "practical" purpose, such as escaping predators (weren't any) or drowning mosquitoes (the day was bugless). It was play for play's sake.

Yet what do such behaviors as these, impressive though they are, really say about whether or not animals possess conscious intellect— the ability to think, reason, plan and act by self-directed choice? Not much, says traditional biology, arguing that even such seemingly spontaneous behaviors as play can be chalked up to "innate tendencies" rather than conscious intent.

So, what *do* the animals know?

It's a lot to think about, and as an avid outdoorsman and student of wild nature, I think about it a lot. Nor am I alone in the pursuit of this beastly koan; people have been pondering the nature and extent of animal consciousness since at least the advent of recorded history, with early students including such cerebral celebrities as Aristotle the Greek and Aesop the fable.

Even so, serious, methodical consideration of animal intelligence didn't really come of its own until the 13th century and the revelations of the Italian Saint Thomas Aquinas. All living things, reasoned St. Tom, have "soul." Animals are more soulful than plants because they (including we) are equipped with sensory organs—eyes, nostrils, ears—through which to gather information about our surroundings. These data subsequently are computed by this mysterious essence called soul and used to act profitably upon the world. The more soulful the animal, the more sophisticated its computation of sensory data until, with humans, soul is sufficiently powerful to facilitate self-awareness, symbolic thought, language, art, science, religion, political sound bytes and all the other "higher qualities" that have brought us to our present state of arrogance, overpopulation, angst, war and woe.

Not such shabby logic, old Tom's, even by today's picky scientific standards, at least if we substitute a contemporary term—say, intellect or thought or consciousness or (getting fancy) cognition—for Aquinas's mystical soul, and doubly impressive considering this was back when the world remained flat and intellectuals debated whether the home of the soul was the heart, brain, liver or some organ more obscure.

Aquinas's placement of the various species on an ascending intellectual scale, like the rungs of a ladder, remained more or less in vogue until the 1600s when animals' souls were rudely repossessed by the French anthropocentrist René ("I think, therefore I am") Descartes, the so-called father of so-called modern philosophy. Echoing the religious dogma of his day, Descartes preached that animals were created expressly for human use and are, by Divine Design, devoid of soul—mere senseless automatons, flesh-and-bone machines, fur-covered robots lacking any shred of consciousness or feeling.

From Descartes's *Discourse on Method:* "There is [no supposition] more powerful in leading feeble minds astray from the straight path of virtue than that the soul of brutes is of the same nature with our own."

Even the agonized screams of beasts in pain, in Descartes's hard-hearted view, were nothing more than the screeches of stressed and damaged machinery.

Handy, this "Cartesian dualism" worldview, with humans as the Chosen Ones of creation and all the rest of nature over on the senseless side of the tracks. Buy into this one, and we have moral license to use and abuse animals any old way we wish, handily unburdened by conscience, empathy or "humanity."

And abuse animals we did, and still do. Consider the assembly line oppression of industrial animal-farming. Consider every American neighborhood's examples of shameful neglect of *Canis familiaris,* "man's best friends," kept caged in small apartments or chained in suburban backyards until they turn loud and mean from neglect and frustration. And consider, please, the living nightmare of vivisection, that blood-splattered circus of Nazi Dr. Doolittle laboratory tortures inflicted on hundreds, perhaps thousands of animals daily ("How smart does a chimp have to be before killing him constitutes murder?" asks the late Carl Sagan), most often for blatantly commercial or scientifically redundant ends rather than to gain vital new medical knowledge.

(Beyond the invisible walls of my sylvan shelter the tempest rages on. The lightning and thunder have jumped the Divide and are moving away, the hail has petered out, but the wind still howls and rain pours with redoubled vigor from a ruptured firmament. And here I squat, carefree as a Caliban.)

Thankfully, all things pass, including René Descartes, whose arrogant old soul now resides in an exclusive heaven where angels sing but hermit thrushes do not and no lowly deer or antelope are allowed to play. Sounds like hell to me. As it did also to most post-Cartesian thinkers, including one Percy Bysshe Shelley, an early 19th century English poet of some modest renown who opined that "The monstrous sophism that beasts are pure unfeeling machines, and do not reason, scarcely requires a confutation."

Likewise, the Scottish philosopher David Hume attacked the Cartesian legacy by asserting that "No truth appears to me more evident than that beasts are endow'd with thought and reason as well as men."

In his turn, the German thinker Arthur Schopenhauer added yet more fuel to the Cartesian funeral pyre with the opinion that even though they lack "true language," animals nonetheless possess conscious understanding and can exert free will.

And so on through a lengthy litany of philosophical opinion, more often than not coming down on the animals' side.

But philosophy, alas, is opinion—albeit thoughtful and elaborately voiced—and fails definitively to answer the query at hand: What do the animals know?

In the 20th century there finally arose a school of serious scientific investigation into animal intelligence, perhaps too serious at times.

Its name was, and remains, behaviorism, and its guru was a psychologist painfully familiar to former students of Psych 101, B. F. Skinner.

Intrigued by the work of that infamous Russian dog trainer "Drooling Ivan" Pavlov, Skinner specialized in tormenting animals with crowded cages, mazes, surgically implanted electrodes and suchlike in hopes of demonstrating, among other things, that for every stimulus (say, cramming more and more rats into a cage), there follows a predictable response (more and more aggression, murder, rape, incest, depression and other familiar urban social ills). Behaviorism came to so dominate the scientific study of animal intelligence that for decades researchers with conflicting ideas and data were reluctant to publish their views for fear of professional ridicule. Hardly the open-minded atmosphere necessary for doing good science.

Only relatively recently has fundamentalist behaviorism finally begun to lose ground to a kinder and gentler school of inquiry called cognitive ethology. Cognition is a fancy word for all that's involved in thought, while ethology is the study of animal behavior under more or less natural (as opposed to harshly clinical) conditions. Nor is it new. As early as the fifth century B.C., a Greek slave writing under the name of Aesop dabbled in cognitive ethology when he celebrated in fable a raven he'd seen dropping small stones into a narrow-necked jug half-full of water, thus displacing and raising the level of the liquid until it could be reached for a drink.

More than two millennia later, in his *Advancement of Learning*, English historian and philosopher Sir Francis Bacon echoed Aesop when he asked rhetorically, "Who taught the raven in a drought to throw pebbles into a hollow tree, where she espied water, that the water might rise so as she could come to it?"

Recent experiments conducted by University of Vermont cognitive ethologist Bernd Heinrich validate the raven's far-flung historical reputation for ingenuity. After suspending a bit of food on a long string below a perch pole, Heinrich photographed one of his birds solving the problem by lifting a length of string with its beak then anchoring the coil to the perch with a foot, over and over again, until it had reeled in the bait. (Crows, on the other hand, never got past grabbing the suspended morsel on the fly, only to have it jerked rudely from their beaks.)

Equally impressive, a second raven, watching the first, didn't merely ape what it saw but improved on the technique by grasping the string loosely in its beak and walking the length of its perch pole to draw it up, thus bringing home the bacon both faster and with considerably less effort.

Similarly, cultural anthropologist Richard K. Nelson, in his celebrated natural history *The Island Within,* reports that ravens are believed by the Koyukon Indians of interior Alaska to lead deserving hunters to game. Having witnessed this fascinating behavior myself, I too have come to view the raven as a hunter's helper. At least on occasion.

Like so: I'm dressed in camouflage and either sitting or creeping quietly through the woods—bowhunting for my winter's meat, photographing wildlife or merely looking—when ravens, usually a pair, appear and circle low overhead, croaking grandly as if saying *Look! Look!* Our relationship thus established, the birds clam up and scram. Then, sooner more often than later, the same ravens sound off again, now from a near distance and in harsher, more urgent tones, repeating a call that I've come to hear as *Elk! Elk!* (In the Koyukon language, says Nelson, it translates as *Animal! Animal!*)

Through conditioning, I've learned to perk up at such times, for once in a while—not often, but often enough to be of serious note— the birds are announcing the whereabouts of elk or deer.

I'm no dreamy-eyed nature mystic and neither is Dr. Nelson. Nor are we suggesting that ravens are attempting to establish some Voodoo New Age connection with humans. Rather, they're simply displaying practical intelligence—working for wages, as it were, in the form of offal and meat scraps left behind by the hunters they help. The conscious intellect implied here—visualizing a profitable end, conceiving a strategy, recognizing and recruiting potential allies, communication, persistence—is food for a lifetime of thought.

On the other hand, as any staunch behaviorist will eagerly testify, innate behavior patterns can provide animals with an impressively broad choice of responses to apparently unique stimuli, leaving unsophisticated observers (like me) with the false impression that thinking has happened.

Certainly, that *can* be the case. But, I wonder, does it have to be either/or? Not in the human beast, with our complex hodgepodge of innate *and* intellectual behaviors. Why always so in other animals? I find it easier to believe that the occasional Einstein raven has intellect enough to purposely join forces with human hunters or conceive the simple dynamics of liquid displacement (although we all know some "normal" *people* who couldn't do either), than to accept that natural selection would bother to imprint such complex and individualized responses in instinct.

For those seriously interested in such arcane corners of nature there are bookfuls of scientifically documented near-human intellectual feats performed by animals of every stripe, from pigeons to primates. In summarizing a few such high points, science writer James Shreeve, in *The Neandertal Enigma*, reminds us that ...

> Given a little training, chimps and gorillas can communicate by using symbols, teach each other sign language and, by some accounts, even discuss their emotions and ideas of death with their trainers. We now know that even in the wild, vervet monkeys utter different alarm cries depending upon what sort of danger is imminent—perhaps the beginning of language. ... Lions hunt cooperatively, wolves share food, elephants regularly display an emotional depth more profound than, say, some modern human beings working on Wall Street.

And also like some modern human beings working on Wall Street, animals are not above deceiving one another for personal gain.

Among the best-documented animal "liars" is the piping plover, which deftly decoys predators away from its ground nests by employing such inventive deceits as flopping off with a faked wing injury or squeaking like a rodent from behind a screen of tall grass—the style of the pretense cleverly tailored to fit the nature of the threat. As long ago as 1833, John James Audubon wrote of the piping plover: "You may see the mother, with expanded tail and wings trailing on the ground, limping and fluttering before you, as if about to expire [but] when the bird has fairly got rid of her unwelcome visitor, and you see her start up on her legs, stretch forth her wings and fly away piping her soft note, you cannot but participate in the joy that she feels."

Similarly, I've had mule deer does and elk cows boldly attempt to decoy me away from their hidden fawns and calves when I've stumbled too close.

James Shreeve touches on the impressively extensive predator-alarm vocabulary of vervet monkeys. Even more impressive is that these fiercely territorial primates employ their "beginning of language" to lie to one another. When a home-team clan of vervets is under attack by an invading clan and the battle seems all but lost, one or more of the defenders may suddenly start screaming the universal vervet equivalent of *Leopard! Run for your lives!* It's the most urgent, frightening and powerful phrase in the vervet repertoire and it invariably sends the invaders packing. No mere monkey business, this, but cunning psychological warfare.

Yet such deceits as the vervet's and plover's are "honorable" lies told not for greedy ends but to protect home and family. More self-serving, and thus more humanlike, are the screeching raptor imitations uttered by Steller's jays as they swoop toward my backyard feeder, effectively clearing the crowded perch of chickadees, nuthatches, juncos and even other jays. Do "selfish" acts such as this not suggest a thoughtful, creative, one might even venture *Machiavellian* intelligence?

Deceit aside, a singularly impressive example of what appears to be high-order animal intellect was related to me by nationally respected black bear biologist Tom Beck. Your standard live-trap for bears consists of a length of large-diameter steel culvert pipe with one end capped shut and the other rigged with a heavy guillotine-type door that slides up between parallel tracks and is held open with a big metal pin. When a bear enters the barrel and tugs the baited trigger mechanism, the pin is pulled, allowing the door to slam shut and trap the bear within.

Says Beck, "I've watched bears who've never seen a culvert trap in their lives walk up to one, check it out from various angles, then stand up, grab the door, and with a powerful twisting motion wrench it sideways to bend and bind it in the open position—then step inside, take the bait and walk away."

This same widely experienced field biologist also reports seeing bears toss rocks or sticks onto the triggers of spring-activated leg snares to fire them off before going in for the goodies. "Bears," Tom Beck will tell you, "appear to be capable of reasoning, planning and spontaneous problem solving."

Seconding Beck is grizzly expert Doug Peacock, who believes grizzly bears are smart enough to know when they're being tracked, are aware of their own footprints and sometimes take pains—such as walking in water or on rocks while avoiding snow and mud—to throw hunters and hounds off their trail, even backtracking to lie in hiding and watch (and, we may presume, chuckle at) their confused pursuers.

And one last anecdote from Beck: In winter, in a shallow creek where the water was frozen solid, he found where a deer had pawed a substantial amount of dirt out onto the ice. Curious, Tom returned the next day and, lo and behold, saw that the deer had been there again to lap up the muddy meltwater. "I'm not saying that deer understand and consciously employ the principles of solar heating," says Beck, "but I do know that a deer intentionally pawed dirt onto ice and the same deer returned later to the same spot to drink from the little pool of water melted by the heat absorbed by the dark-colored dirt."

Even so—all these feats of apparent animal intelligence and plenty more notwithstanding—it remains that without true language with which to share and expand whatever knowledge they possess, animals are doomed (or blessed) never to enjoy (or endure) the abstract mental abilities that define the human mind (just try thinking without words). Some theorists even venture that language *is* consciousness.

What do the animals know?

Wild animals, above all and beyond argument, know The Secret of Life (as did we, for some three million years before biting the forbidden fruit and taking the Big Wrong Turn into intensive agriculture), as proven by their ability to exist in perpetual balance (if not always harmony) with their fellow creatures and the environment that sustains us all. It's a basic, absolutely essential quality of intelligence that *Homo saps* seem destined never to acquire.

But ask now the beasts, and they shall teach thee; and the fowls of the air and they shall tell thee. Or speak to the earth, and it shall teach thee.

Fat chance, Job.

∾

As suddenly as it appeared, the wind now dies. The rain fizzles and stops. And thanks to the practical intellect of the cud-chewing ungulate that pawed out this sheltered nest I'm squatting in, I've ridden out a horrendous storm sans raingear and am sitting pretty—pretty dry, pretty warm, pretty comfortable, pretty grateful. Intelligence, I reflect, is what works best to satisfy a species' needs in the niche in which it finds itself. I mean—what use would an elk have for a Ph.D.?

It has been suggested that even if we could find some way to talk with the animals, what they had to say would be Greek to us, so different is their perception and "processing" of the world from our own. All the thoughts of a turtle are turtle, surmised Emerson. If so, why then do we persist in trying to decipher animal intelligence based on the human model?

So many questions, so few answers.

∼

I stand and stumble out through the dark dripping trees and back into the big montane meadow where my halcyon day hike was so rudely interrupted some hours ago. Night has slammed down hard and black as obsidian, erasing all landmarks and shifting my mood from philosophical to paranoid: Where the hell *am* I, and which way back to camp?

From somewhere out in the inky void rises an eerie fluted wail followed by a staccato series of braying chuckles. My temporarily evicted wapiti host, I suppose, enjoying the last laugh. My navigational quandary aside, I have to smile. The bull elk's bugle, like the down-scale crescendo of the canyon wren, is a language imbued with more mystery, magic, passion and *sustainable* intellect than we space-walking humans can ever hope to comprehend. That beast out there is already home, while I have yet to find my way.

8

A Hunter's Heart

SEPTEMBER. The most august of months here in the southern Rockies. The flies and mosquitoes are gone, most of them, as are the buzzing swarms of motorized tourists. Autumn aspens illuminate the landscape with an ancient golden light. Days are sunny and t-shirt warm, nights crisp and star-spangled.

Better yet, September is rut: mating season for the wily wapiti. The valleys ring with the urgent bugles of love-struck bulls, and the pungent incense of their fierce animal lust perfumes the mountain air. It's an otherworldly music, the bull elk's bugle, a calamitous crescendo of brassy high notes proclaiming a wildness we can hardly imagine.

It's still dark when I wheel into a little-used trailhead at the end of a ragged dirt road bisecting a local parcel of land owned by the Colorado Division of Wildlife. As the sun also rises I buckle into my oversized backpack, lock my truck (oh yes, even here) and take the trail less traveled. My plan is to rendezvous with a young friend—a former student back when I was an English teacher at the local college—at his hide-away hunting camp ... somewhere *out there*. The way from here to there is new to me and, Lane has forewarned, "real up." Once there, I'll have all the time in the world (relatively speaking) to enjoy the bugling bulls, the gilded whispering aspens, a sedom-seen friend's companionship and as much mountain solitare as I wish.

Onward.

Although this state-owned parcel is only a few miles from my frenetic, tourist-trampled, realtor-infested hometown of Durango, the 6900-acre foothill tract is refuge for peregrine falcons, eagles both golden and bald, wild turkeys, black bears, cougars, mule deer, elk and more. Deer, elk and their predators, especially, rely on this place and a dwindling few more like it hereabouts to sustain them through the long and often brutal Colorado winters in these "economically healthy" times of rampant rapine.

Until a handful of years ago, the Animas River valley, anchored dead center by Durango, remained blissfully undiscovered by ex-urban yupsters and the real estate whores who follow them like fleas, retaining its traditional agrarian nature and providing wildlife with abundant wintering areas in low-lying ranch pastures, especially along the cottonwood-sheltered riparian corridor of the river itself. (*Rio de las Animas Perdidas*, River of Lost Souls; an apropos name, that, given the way things are going around here.)

But discovered it eventually was, and every year more traditional wildlife habitat is reduced to obscene, energy-squandering trophy houses for the conspicuous and uncultured new-rich, redundant water-guzzling golf courses (three on the ground and a fourth on the drawing board), tacky commercial and industrial parks, noisy (un)-natural gas fields and seas of suburban subdivisions to hold a flood-tide of West Coast refugees that shows no sign of ebbing.

The "Grow or die!" chamber-of-commerce hacks call it progress.

The animals call it hard times.

I call it heartbreaking.

Looking around me now as I hike through this severely stressed elk wintering ground, the signs of pending disaster are ubiquitous: The brushy little Gambel's oak, whose acorns and annual twig growth sustain a plethora of winter wildlife, have been cropped almost to their trunks. Not just here and there, but everywhere. Too many elk and not enough elk chow. Come the next killer winter (and come it will; it's overdue even now), this wildlife "refuge" will become a showplace of suffering, a cervid dying field. Progress.

But hey, Petersen, lighten up; we're on vacation here.

In due time I leave the state land behind and cross some rancher's "bob-war" fence onto a cow-burned corner of adjoining private land. After an hour or so more of steady marching I cross another fence and enter the San Juan National Forest, where the faint cutoff path I've been following intersects a broad backwoods freeway known as the Colorado Trail. Were I to turn downtrail rather than up, the CT would deliver me in due course to one of the most popular trailheads for mountain bikers this side of the Land of the Moabites.

And sure enough, within minutes, here come a pack of riders— three young studs, skull-capped and body-painted in Lycra, their legs tumescent from pumping like pistons on toys worth more than my investments portfolio. They give no indication of seeing me, though surely they must, and show no inclination to slow down, so that at the last possible moment I'm forced to leap off the trail or be thrice clobbered. As the pack speeds past, I wave them a single-digit farewell.

Shaken, I step back onto the trail and continue my uphill journey, breathing deeply, rhythmically, invoking a respiratory mantra intended to cool my boiling blood. Trail encounters between bikers and hikers don't have to be this rude, and it disturbs me that they so often are. One potential source of friction, I suppose, is that mountain bikers tend to view themselves as competitive athletes and, consequently, are more focused on the performance of their equipment and themselves, and the relative positions of their competitor-companions, than on the surroundings through which they race in a sweat-slinging blur. Hikers, on the other hand, prefer contemplation to competition, scenery to speed. The irony, I realize, is that a hiker one day may be a biker another. In outdoor recreation as in other endeavors, the activity often dictates the personality.

Time passes, as do the slow steep miles. The oak brush thickets and open, sunny ponderosa woods of the lower montane ecology gradually are supplanted by cool dark forests of spruce and fir bejeweled with flickering groves of quaking aspens. All around me now, millions of loose-jointed leaves answer to the midmorning breeze, whispering sibilant secrets in an ancient alien tongue.

And with the aspens come frequent signs, and occasional sightings, of the wild menagerie that thrives among the shady groves' fecund understory of ferns, giant cow parsnips, angelica, chokecherry, serviceberry and a frenzy of mountain wildflowers. Already this morning I've interrupted two conventions of big blue grouse as they pecked for brunch in the leafy duff. (The grouse hunting season is open and I'm carrying the proper license, but I'm not hunting right now, I'm hiking.) A little farther along I'm treated to the pigeon-toed prints of an adult black bear. The heart-shaped tracks of deer and elk are everywhere and the forest is alive with the happy chatter of birds and … damn, I knew it was too good to last.

Fifty yards ahead, loping easily downtrail, talking and laughing, come three brethren backpackers—no, one brethren and two sistern. This time I am not forced, as I was with the speeding cyclists, but freely elect to step off the narrow trail and make way. The hikers see me and—to my surprise, rather than offering greetings—fall suddenly silent. When they come abreast I smile and say good-day and am thoroughly nonplused when they keep right on marching, their replies limited to a Hi and a Hello from the women, a silent somber nod from the man. A triple cold shoulder. Not that I care.

Or do I? Granted, in my middle ages I'm no longer quite so pretty as I once never was, but even so, I can't imagine that I'm in any way threatening.

The mystery is solved a few moments later when one of the women—they've rounded a bend and must think they're out of earshot—says, "A *hunter!*" hurling the word like a curse. After that I can hear no more, and just as well.

I should have known. Although I'm hiking in shorts and lugging a bulging backpack, I'm also wearing a camouflaged shirt and cap and carrying a bow and quiver of arrows. Today I'm no mere harmless backpacker, I'm "a *hunter!*" Or at least I hope to be if I ever get where I'm going.

The more I reflect on this, the more it bugs me, notwithstanding I harbor judgmental generalizations of my own. Hikers, bikers, hunters, fishers, horse people, boaters, birdwatchers, photographers—we're all out here for the same root reason—to enjoy *being out here,* albeit each in our own way. Further, we frequently play musical outdoor-activity chairs (with the exception of biker, I am at one time and another each of the above). It's just too damn bad that our gear, dress and mindset for a particular day's excursion so often seem to dictate—not just the attitudes of others toward us, but the attitudes we ourselves project. Protean role playing.

My map tells me I'm nearing the ten-thousand-foot contour and my stomach tells me it's lunch time. Today's menu (and tomorrow's, and the next day's): dried fruit, a big slab of homemade elk jerky, a chocolate bar and a quart of tepid water. I collapse in the shade, jettison my sweaty pack, eat, drink and shift into mental neutral. A nap tries to ambush me, but there are unknown miles left to hike and the sun is past its apogee, so after half an hour I groan to my feet, saddle up and stagger back out into the brilliant heart of a perfect September day, rejoicing in my solitude.

For a little while, at least—ten minutes or so—when here comes yet more traffic. (This unrelenting, unwanted *society* is starting to wear thin.) Wonderful, another mountain biker, this one apparently alone, catching a free down-trail ride on gravity. I brace for the usual brusque encounter, but this day is made for surprises and the young man brakes to a stop and awaits my approach. "Hi," he says as I draw near, smiling big and real. "You must be Dave. I'm Bill. Lane told me to watch for you."

Now what the hell.

Though Bill is dressed in *de rigueur* biker black, I see now that he too is a hunter, his short compound bow strapped across the bars, and bundles of camping gear appended everywhere. Bill tells me that he's just come from two days of camping and hunting with Lane. Now it's back to Denver and work for him while Lane ("that lucky bum") stays on for a full vacation week. Lane had advised me that a friend of his would be leaving camp the same day I'd be arriving and we might cross paths, but I hadn't expected a biker.

With no further ado, Bill offers to ride back up the trail with me— "just a couple of miles"—to set me on the obscure elk path (just one of hundreds bisecting the interminable Colorado Trail) that will lead me, after a mile or so of bushwhacking, to Lane's cloistered camp. I protest that it's too much trouble. Bill counters that I'll never find it on my own, then dumps the bulk of his stuff alongside the trail, wheels around, gears down and pedals slowly, almost effortlessly back up the mountain. I follow at a fast, heart-pounding lope, painfully aware that this blows hell out of my bikers-as-buttheads stereotype.

Arrived at the invisible cut-off, Bill wishes me good luck and disappears. I leave the crowded CT without remorse and follow the serpentine, blowdown-clogged game trail until it peters out on a narrowing tongue of wooded ridge, where I find ... nothing. No camp in sight. As pre-arranged, I take a small plastic disc from my shirt pocket, place it against the roof of my mouth and blow, producing a mew that sounds not unlike a lost kitten.

Silence.

I repeat the elk coalescence call and this time receive an in-kind reply from the shadowy forest below. I stumble down that way and right into Lane's cloistered camp.

For what's left of the afternoon we catnap and talk. Come evening, we boil pure Rocky Mountain creek water to rehydrate our desiccated dinners. As dark approaches, the temperature drops in harness with the sun, prompting Lane to kindle a campfire I feel compelled to comment is "pretty damned thrifty."

"Well," Lane defends, "I usually camp cold when I'm hunting. Don't want to scare the animals away, you know. But it's chilly tonight, so what the heck ... but we'll keep it small."

I'd have said "what the hell," but Lane is a fundamentalist Christian and rarely swears. I too am religious, but in a radically different sense, which philosophical diversity leads to some fairly high-flown, occasionally high-tension campfire dialogue. ("Nature," muses Lane, "is God's grandest creation." "Nature," I counter, stealing a line from my anthropologist friend Richard Nelson, "*is* God.")

Over tea (he) and whiskey (me), we cuss (me) and discuss (he) my day's troubling trail encounters. The macho young bikers, we agree—well, boys will be pricks, especially when running in gangs; to hell with them. More difficult to figure and far more bothersome is the behavior of that trio of hikers. I'm sure, I tell Lane, that my meeting with them would have been warmer had I not been carrying a bow and arrows. Why is that?

"Well," says Lane, "maybe they've had bad experiences with hunters in the past. Hunters are people, and a lot of people are slobs in everything they do and its human nature to draw negative generalizations from a few bad individuals."

Right you are. I consider my own biases—against mountain bikers, public lands ranchers (a coalescence of scoundrels), New Mexico drivers (the only requirement for an operator's license there, it seems, is a prefrontal lobotomy) and other groups with whose members I've had repeated unpleasant run-ins.

"But what," I abruptly offer, looking to justify my own unjustifiable prejudices, "what of Sartre's *le pour-soi* and *l'en-soi?* What of *that* little distinction my man, eh?"

"Nor," continues my young friend, adroitly dodging my non sequitur and steering us back on track, "nor does the negative image of hunting that's put out by the popular media help any. It seems that only slob hunters, wildlife criminals and animal rights fanatics are newsworthy."

"Seems so," I grant, recalling the devastatingly out-of-context teevee documentary *The Guns of Autumn*; the joyfully bitchy (and, I must admit, clever) outbursts (in *Esquire* and elsewhere) of a certain (to borrow Jim Harrison's description) "minor regional novelist," et al. and so on.

"But it's not only the news and popular media who distort hunting," I propose. "Just as bad are the hook-and-bullet rags who've sold their souls for advertising dollars, and the industry-sponsored self-proclaimed 'hunters' rights' propaganda groups with their half-truths, entrenched denial and paranoid right-wing ranting about 'the growing antihunting threat.' With a few sterling exceptions, the hunting media and hunters' groups are so far right they make Limbaugh look left. The pro-gun, ostensibly pro-hunting politicians they're helping to elect are the same sonsabitches who are helping industry confiscate and despoil what little remains of America's public wildlands. And without a *place* to hunt, hunting's dead no matter how many hunters' 'rights' we have or assault rifles and Saturday night specials we own. 'To preserve wild animals implies generally the creation of a forest for them to dwell in or resort to.' Thoreau said that over a century ago, and it's the simplest, most self-evident sort of logic—yet a lot of hunters *still* don't get it."

On a streak—were Caroline here, she'd call it a rampage—I knock back another slash of Dickel-and-branch, torch up a good plebeian Swisher Sweet and lunge ahead.

"The greatest threat to hunting isn't the antis, old buddy; it's us and our collective failure to police our own ranks and morals. There's a lot wrong with hunting today, and I don't mean just illegal activities like poaching. The root problem is the hunting community's hard-headed refusal to admit that some things some hunters do, even when legal, are ethically indefensible: baiting, using hounds to tree bears and mountain lions then executing them like bass in buckets, rich-man's globe-trotting head-hunting, canned 'hunts' for exotic imported species on fenced Texas 'game ranches,' rampant littering and ATV abuse, road 'hunting,' contest killing, employing space-age technology to minimize challenge, dead animals conspicuously displayed on vehicles, political alignment with the no-compromise far-right radical militia mentality, anti-environment voting and a general care-less-ness in our behavior afield."

Lane nods in silent agreement.

"Increasingly," I drone on, a little tipsy now, "these sins are dividing our ranks, forcing ethical hunters to become nonhunters, converting nonhunters to antihunters, lowering the recruitment of new hunters and providing powerful ammunition to the rabid hunter-haters. What was it Twain said? 'Ain't we got all the fools in town on our side, and ain't that majority enough anywhere?' Hunting today is fat with fools; it's a built-in flaw of democracy— any idiot can do any damn thing he wants in America, so long as it's marginally legal. Modern hunting is badly in need of a good internal bullshit filter. We need ..."

"Now *just* a darn minute," says Lane, feigning (I think) outrage. "You know danged well that there's an increasingly powerful political lobby of loony-tunes animal rights fanatics out there, urban innocents who fantasize a Rousseauvian world where *all* predation, human *and* animal, is eliminated, where cougars lie down with fawns and wildlife populations are kept in check with contraceptives. These turkeys have sworn to stop *all* hunting, not just the bad bits. And most of them are so blissfully ignorant of how the natural world works they couldn't tell a deer from a steer if it was standing on their Birkenstocks. Their arguments are biologically naive, unworkable and ultimately immoral."

All right, Lane! My earnest opponent stops just long enough to fortify himself with the dregs of his tea, then bulls ahead.

"What the fanatical animal rights types refuse to acknowledge is that humans evolved as hunter-gatherers, as predators; and nature *needs* predation, especially these days. With most of the big natural predators wiped out to make the world safe for our brainless domesticated livestock, and with more and more wild ungulates being crammed into less and less habitat, hunters, as ironic as it may sound to the uninformed, have become wildlife's closest allies."

No argument. I think of those state wildlife lands down the mountain. If it weren't for money extracted from hunters through license fees and excise taxes, that land would be just another subdivision. Guaranteed. Overcrowded it may be, but at least it's *there,* thanks entirely to hunters. Yet, such pragmatic justifications of hunting fail

to bear on the opposition's primary complaints, which are philosophical, not utilitarian.

Musing along these lines, I recall a story related to me by David
Stalling, conservation editor for *Bugle*, the journal of the Rocky
Mountain Elk Foundation. While backpack bowhunting in the Idaho
wilderness recently, Stalling encountered a couple of hikers. The men
identified themselves as attorneys for a major environmental group,
out to enjoy some of the wilderness they worked daily (at West Coast
lawyer wages) to protect. Across the next half hour, the two back-
packing barristers derided, berated and verbally excoriated Stalling
with the pious conviction only lawyers and preachers can muster. For
why? For being a hunter. Dave says he attempted to answer their
charges calmly and reasonably, but they were having none of it; their
minds were closed and their mouths wide open.

Finally, tiring of the game, Stalling wished his critics a good day
and walked on. "Wait a minute!" one of the pair called after him.
"Listen—we're kind of ... well, *lost*; can you tell us how to get *out of
here?*" Dave, a former Marine Corps recon ranger, pulled out his
topographical maps and showed them the way. I doubt that I could
have been so generous.

(It was also David Stalling, I recall with admiration, who recently
wrote the words that have become my personal mantra: "We don't
need *more* hunters, we need *better* hunters." Thus he refutes legions
of industry hacks who would have us believe that "If hunting is to
survive, we need all the hunters we can get." Yes, of course we do, and
the fact that all those hunters will buy lots of *stuff* has nothing to do
with it, does it boys?)

Lane's chintzy little fire flickers, flares and fades to cherry embers.
Likewise, our conversation, recently so lively, has given way to silent
introspection—and we never even got around to the real meat of the
matter, the hardest question of all: the paradox of finding great pleasure in an activity whose end goal is death, while claiming to care
deeply about the very animals we work so earnestly to kill.

But such refined rhetoric will have to wait for another evening, another so-called campfire. Lane and I rise and stagger tentward. With no bugs or Bubbas buzzing about to annoy us, we decide to sleep with the tent flaps tied back and our heads poking out, the better to enjoy the sparkling firmament.

"I should probably warn you," says Lane as he zips into his sack (*Oh no,* I'm thinking, *the bum snores!*), "There's been something weird hanging around here the past couple of nights, making the eeriest noises you've ever heard. When it came last night, Bill and I got up and shined our flashlights all around, but it went quiet and we never saw it. Sort of spooky."

I haven't a clue.

Sometime after midnight I'm awakened by a sharp jab on the shoulder. "It's back. Listen!" I listen, and sure enough, before long comes a loud, ethereal keening, like some demented demon's spawn in need of a diaper change. Real close.

"What the hell *is* it?" whispers Lane, forgetting for once to not cuss.

The banshee wails again, this time in stereo, and suddenly I know. "Porcupines," I say. "Making love."

"Well," says Lane, clearly relieved, "I'll be danged."

ᘏ

Thanks to the amorous porkies, we oversleep, waking only when the sun slaps our faces. In penance we forego coffee, bolt some elk jerky and swig some creek water for breakfast, grab our bows and strike off for adventures unknown. This entire huge basin is *terra incognita* to me, and Lane has generously volunteered to conduct an orienting tour.

During a laconic morning of quiet poking around, we find where elk have recently foraged and where their big cloven hooves have sunk deep in the mud of a spring seep. By examining their droppings—the older turds (hard and sun-bleached) are in the shape of formless lumps, like modest cow pies, while the fresher (soft and shiny black) poops resemble acorns—by studying these we determine that the big herbivores are already shifting from their soft spring and summer fare of grasses and forbs to a fall and winter diet of woody browse.

And suchlike other bits of woodslore that only field biologists and serious hunters ever bother to notice.

The high point of the morning comes when our noses lead us to a fresh wallow carved into a muddy spring seep, proving that at least one mature bull is lurking hereabouts, probably shaded-up close by even now, chewing contemplative cud and watching, listening, nostrils flared for danger. I drop to my knees for a closer reading of the spoor.

The story is clearly written: Some sex-crazed male has hooved the spring seep into a quagmire, urinated into the mucky mess, stirred it around then rolled in it to cake himself with the funky perfume—the wapiti way of dressing for a hot date. Nearby, a forlorn spruce sapling has been stripped of its bark and lower limbs by the hormone-enraged bull's aggressive horning.

I put my face down close to the reeking wallow and inhale deep of its pungent, pheromone-laden essence, prompting my wiseacre friend to quip, "Why'nt ya just roll in it and experience the real *essence* of elkness?"

I don't bother to mention that I've tried that, back in my formative years as an elkoholic. A horrendous error.

It's early afternoon when we sag back into camp for lunch and naps. Later, we fling a few practice arrows at a makeshift target, check the sharpness of our broadheads and otherwise make ready for a serious evening hunt.

Lane's plan, he announces, is to climb a nearby promontory and bugle. Any rutting bull within hearing (so the theory goes) will interpret the calls as a challenge to his territorial dominance and answer in kind, revealing his location. Might even come a'running, hot for a scuffle. More often, though, a vocally challenged harem bull will simply herd up his cows and run away (to live and breed another day). But even a retreating bull will often bugle, granting the hunter the priceless gift of hearing him sing. Bottom line: You never know; occasionally the magic works, far more often it doesn't. Which is exactly as it should be. To paraphrase Spanish philosopher José Ortega y Gasset, hunting should always be problematical.

Lane invites me to join him, yet seems relieved when I decline. For Lane, as for me and many another serious hunter, playing the silent, solitary predator is the quintessential outdoor experience; companionship and conversation are best saved for the evening campfire (be it ever so humble).

We exchange good lucks and Lane strikes off uphill. I go low, headed back to a grassy little glen at the bottom of a nearby canyon where food, water and wooded seclusion—the Big Three of quality wildlife habitat—are concentrated in one of the spots where we cut fresh sign this morning. There to lie in ambush. Elk or no, it's a room with a view.

Time passes in restful quietude, and less than an hour of light remains when I hear a high, clean, distant call that rises through three octaves, sustains briefly, then comes crashing back to earth. Assuming (as I do) that it's Lane and not the genuine article, he's probably a mile away as the arrow flies.

No sooner has Lane's realistic fake bugle faded than I hear, much nearer, a low grunt and a brittle crashing of limbs. Adrenaline surges and my heart slams into overdrive. The sounds are coming from a wooded plateau directly across my little canyon, and I don't have to see the noise-maker to know who it is and what he's up to—a wapiti bull, infuriated by Lane's vocal challenge, is venting his outrage in barely restrained semi-silence, stomping the ground and antler-thrashing some unfortunate tree.

When Lane bugles again, the bull looses his cool and fires back immediately. The animal is close enough, a hundred yards or so, that I can hear not only the shrillest high notes of his call, but the deep, guttural, underlying growls as well. Lane sings a third time and the bull, by now hot as a bootleg firecracker, replies with a series of five rapid, braying grunts, which I interpret to mean: *Yo momma, sucker!*

And here I sit, masticating my options. I could enter the fray with a bugle or cow chirp of my own. That might bring the bull out of hiding and into the self-imposed twenty-yard range of my naked little stick bow. Might also scare him plumb out of the neighborhood. My only other choice is to try to stalk within range without getting busted. But only lovers, fools and inexperienced hunters rush in, and if I move as slowly and painstakingly as I should, as I must, I'll run out of daylight before I get there.

"Problematical" indeed. That's why we call it *hunting.*

Well, tomorrow is another day, another opportunity. Resigned to temporary defeat, I place my weapon on the ground beside me and lie back against the cool, leaf-cushioned earth to enjoy the sunset concert. Short of a miracle of luck, there will be no killing this night.

But the *hunting* could hardly be better.

ᦓ

Why do I hunt?

It's a lot to think about, and I think about it a lot. I hunt to acknowledge my evolutionary roots, countless millennia deep, as a predatory omnivore. To participate actively in the grand play of nature. For the atavistic challenge of doing it well with an absolute minimum of technological assistance. To learn the lessons, about nature and myself, that only hunting can teach. To accept personal responsibility for at least some of the deaths that nourish my life. For the glimpse hunting, and only hunting, offers into a wildness we can hardly imagine. Because it provides the closest thing I've ever had to a spiritual experience. Because it reminds me that *I am animal.*

I hunt because Man evolved to hunt, because it gets me *out here* when nothing else will (the importance of which the ever-eloquent Ortega y Gasset states as *Yo soy yo y mi circunstancia*: "I am I and my surroundings") ... because the hyper-alertness demanded by true hunting is the original natural high (Ortega's "mystical agitation") ... because, all sum, hunting enriches my life ... because I was born with a hunter's heart.

PART THREE

Voices in the Wilderness

9

Where Phantoms Come to Brood and Mourn

A Tribute to Edward Paul Abbey: 1927–1989

There is a valley in the West where phantoms come to brood and
mourn, pale phantoms dying of nostalgia and bitterness. You can hear
them, shivering, chattering, among the leaves of the old dry mortal
cottonwoods down by the river—whispering and moaning and hissing
with the wind ... whining their past away with the wild dove and the
mockingbird—and you may see one, touch one, in the silences and
space and mute terror of the desert.
                    —Edward Abbey from *The Brave Cowboy*

MARCH 14, THE ANNIVERSARY of Edward Abbey's premature death.
Ed was a writer, of course, a damned good one, and the godfather of
so-called radical environmentalism. But this isn't about either of
those things.

I'm sitting in the desert sand beside Abbey's hidden grave, talking
and joking and weeping with him, and smoking a cheap cigar—not
the kind he preferred, but the kind he smoked a lot of; even for the
"Thoreau of the American West" (actually, he was better than that),
life was often a compromise. It has been a pilgrimage, or as close to
one as I'll likely ever come, this visit to the last refuge of the man I
respected and loved more than any other. And befitting a true pilgrimage, the way here has not been easy.

∾

After a tiring road trip, my guide and I veer off the blacktop and stop. I get out and lock in my old truck's four-by-four hubs and we go grinding down a sandy desert two-track. A long time later, we stop again and set camp. The rest of the way will be afoot.

As I swig water and otherwise prepare for a desert hike, my guide kneels and scratches a map in the sun-warmed sand, points westward, speaks a few soft words. From here, by choice, I'm on my own. It's at least an hour's fast hike over prickly, unfamiliar terrain, she says. With little more than two hours of daylight left, I step out briskly.

I must be vague in this narrative. The shrine I'm seeking is on public land and no burial permit was applied for; nor, most likely, would one have been granted. Ed needs his privacy. I am sworn, therefore, to a pact of secrecy.

And it's really best this way. By being nowhere in particular, Edward Abbey, whose writing and personal example has meant so much to so many, is now everywhere in spirit, ubiquitous, universalized, happily haunting every slickrock promontory, every slot canyon, every cedar-scented mesa, every hidden valley, every wild place remaining in the American Southwest. If you know about Abbey, if you've read *Desert Solitaire, The Monkey Wrench Gang, The Fool's Progress, Confessions of a Barbarian* or any other of Ed's two-dozen books, then you know the sort of place I'm so carefully not describing here. Abbey Country.

I stride on, dividing my attention between the ground approaching my boots and the rocky, ragged horizon. The afternoon is warm but hardly hot; eighty, maybe. Perfect.

Half an hour out, a shadow like a B-52 slips across the ground ahead of me, crossing from right to left. I stop and look up. Between me and a blinding sun, a huge dark form glides in easy spirals on a thermal whirlpool. I look down for a moment, then squint my eyes and glance again at the indistinct, haloed silhouette. An eagle, possibly. Too big for hawk, raven or falcon. Nor is it likely a turkey buzzard; the wings lack sufficient dihedral, the tail is too broadly fanned. Too bad. How appropriate it would be just now if that *were* a scuzzy old vulture milling around up there—Abbey's afterlife alter ego.

"Given a choice," Ed wrote in "Watching the Birds,"

> I plan to be a long-winged fantailed bird next time around. Which one? Vulture, eagle, hawk, falcon, crane, heron, wood ibis? Well, I believe I was a wood ibis once, back in the good old days of the Pleistocene epoch. And from what I already know of passion, violence, the intensity of the blood, I think I'll pass on eagle, hawk or falcon this time. For a lifetime or two, or maybe three, I think I'll settle for the sedate career, serene and soaring, of the humble turkey buzzard. ... And contemplate this world we love from a silent and considerable height.

Alas, the longwinged fan-tailed bird up there contemplating this particular bit of the world from a silent and considerable height is no vulture. And just as well, I suppose. Like Ed himself acknowledged toward the end of his avian musings, "As appealing as I find the idea of reincarnation, I must confess that it has a flaw: to wit, there is not a shred of evidence suggesting it might be true."

Anyhow, my big bird, of whatever feather, is deserting me, fading fast into the glaring west, chasing the sun down the afternoon sky.

And I had best get on with my own chase.

My boots pick up the pace until the rough-and-tumble terrain is flowing past in a soft blur. Flat to gently rolling, this is hiking heaven compared to the uphill-both-ways mountains of home. Even so, hiking here is complicated by a litter of sharp-edged rocks and a plague of cacti and other prickly desert vegetation, necessitating constant vigilance and frequent dodging, providing plenty of opportunity to stub a toe, twist an ankle, stumble and fall, maybe trod upon an indolent rattler. Hiking out across here with just a light pack, as I am now, is one thing, but lugging a six-foot-three, 180-pound man any distance over this natural obstacle course would be something else entirely.

Yet a fistful of good and loyal friends did exactly that, honoring Ed's wishes to be "transported in the bed of a pickup truck and buried as soon as possible after death. No undertakers wanted, no embalming (for godsake!), no coffin. Just an old sleeping bag. … I want my body to help fertilize the growth of a cactus, or cliffrose, or sagebrush or tree."

While he was about it, Ed had some fun arranging his own wake, calling for bagpipes, a bonfire, "a flood of beer and booze! Lots of singing, dancing, talking, hollering, laughing and love-making. No formal speeches desired, though if someone feels the urge, the deceased will not interfere."

Ed got all of that and more at what was surely the biggest party Saguaro National Monument (now park) has ever seen. I spent most of the day prostrate in the stingy shade of a paloverde tree—stoned in the morning, drunk in the afternoon—trying my best, like the other hundred and more mourners there, to smile and laugh and deny the mutual tragedy that had brought us together. No matter that Ed had assured us "it is not death or dying which is tragic, but rather to have existed without fully participating in life—that is the deepest personal tragedy."

Edward Abbey suffered his share of life's tragedies. But lack of active participation was not among them. He had fun.

I'm occasionally asked what the "real" Edward Abbey was like: Did the laughing, farting, animate *man* bear any resemblance to "Cactus Ed," the eloquently gruff, gloriously ornery literary persona of his autobiographical prose?

I'd say the two were essentially identical. Not even Abbey the writer could invent a character as colorful, complex and contradictory as Abbey the man. The Edward Abbey I knew was quiet, joyful and easygoing most of the time but fierce in argument, alternately sensitive and crass as dictated by company and circumstance, the perfect gentleman if he thought you deserved it, a loving husband and father, a loyal and generous friend, impossible to pigeon-hole.

But I entered the picture on the final reel, and there had been an Edward Abbey I never knew—the young restless quixotic version. That Abbey, on the road to becoming the Ed I knew, had known his share of troubles, most of them of the flirty-skirty type. "How can I be true to just one woman," he would feign to ponder, grinning slyly, "without being untrue to all the rest?"

You were no saint, Ed, thank the gods.

Lost in these musings, time and distance pass quickly and after an hour of speed-hiking I'm standing atop the promontory near where I've been told Ed is holed up these days, relaxing in his favorite sleeping bag. I survey the scene—a large, flat-topped expanse of rock, sand, cactus—then walk to a place that looks more or less right. And there I find ... rock, sand, cactus. The perfection of nothingness.

Hunch having failed me, I decide to try a pinch of method, and spend the next several minutes pacing back and forth across the promontory in something loosely approximating a grid search. *Nada.*

Time grows short. Fifteen minutes more and I'll be wandering around out here like Moses when the lights went off. Just me, the bats, the owls and, somewhere. ...

I'm admiring a sunset as beautiful and ineffable as life itself, pondering where to search next, dusk creeping over the land and shadowing my hopes, when I hear the lonesome cooing of a mourning dove. The melancholy music rises from somewhere beyond the promontory's rim, down a slope that drops off toward a desert valley spreading south and west beyond sight—broad, barren, eerie as hell beneath the deep-purple twilight. No roads, no buildings, no lights down there. Only a pure, clean, peaceful emptiness—the way I imagine death.

Without questioning the impulse, I go skidding and sliding down the slope, homing on the calling dove. And why not? At this point, one direction seems as good as another, and the sunset view from down there should be superb. As I draw noisily near, the mourner falls silent and wings away, a ghostly gray shadow dissolving into the gloaming.

Fighting back creeping despair, determined to search through the night if necessary—I have water, fruit, matches, compass, a windbreaker and flashlight in my pack, and the weather is sublime—I turn and start back up the slope, bumbling blindly through the dying minutes of the day ... and bumble hard into a low-lying cactus, kicking a trident of nettlesome spines through the thin nylon of my boot top and deep into my left foot.

After breaking off all three brittle shafts in a clumsy, half-panicked attempt to rid myself of their searing pain, I'm forced to sit down and unlace and delicately remove the boot, peel back the sock and painstakingly extract the hot-barbed tips. Somewhere off in the shadows, a coyote laughs at my predicament.

Only now—throbbing in self-inflicted torture, one shoe off and one shoe on like some dippy nursery rhyme character, mumbling disparagements at myself for not paying more attention to where my feet were landing, cursing the coyote for his arrogant and insensitive scorn—only now do I look up and see, no more than six feet from my sunburned nose, native rock the size of a badger and bearing a neatly chiseled inscription, which I squint to read in the failing light:

EDWARD

PAUL

ABBEY

1927–1989

NO COMMENT

So and at last it has come to pass that I am sitting here in the desert sand beside an old friend's hidden grave, talking and joking and weeping with him, and smoking a cheap cigar. What's left of it.

"No Comment" ... that was Ed's reply when asked by his old friend Jack Loeffler if he had any last words for posterity. A joker to the end, that Abbey.

Life sure gets strange sometimes. I like to think of myself as a down-to-earth realist. Mysticism is not my magic. Yet, here I sit in a remote sundown desert, dumbfounded by the double coincidence of dove call and cactus spine that would seem to have pointed me here—which *did* lead me here—to this place I've wanted and needed for so long to be. The timing of the coyote's laugh ... it would be easy, almost tempting, to *not* dismiss it all as mere coincidence, given the powerful circumstances.

"Do you believe in ghosts?" Ed once asked himself in his journals, answering, "Those that haunt the human soul, yes." In that respect, at least, I am truly haunted. Beyond that, it's hard to know *what* to think just now.

But I do know what Ed would think, what he'd say (I almost said, "were he here") about the eerie coincidence of events and this superstitious line of thought I'm following. He'd grin that lupine grin of his, shrug and offer, "Who knows? Who cares? And what difference does it make anyway?"

Good questions, Ed.

I mouth the stump of my deceased cigar, stare at the modest headstone—perfect—and fall to musing, casting back across the precious little time I was privileged to spend with Edward Paul Abbey, the man whose fellow writers (he had no peers) have called "brash, irresponsibly satiric, happily excessive ... a full-blooded man ... a man 'still with the bark on' ... a man of character and courage ... the original fly in the ointment ... a gadfly with a stinger like a scorpion ... a rebel and an eloquent loner ... a national treasure" ... and occasionally, by those lacking the open-minded intelligence to stay with him, things far less generous.

∽

The last time I saw Ed Abbey was just after Thanksgiving, 1988. He, his wife Clarke and their lap-sized children Becky and Ben had sardined themselves into the cab of Ed's old Ford pickup and driven the five hundred miles from Tucson up to Durango.

They had come for a book signing at Maria's, an elegant (Ed's term) little Southwest-flavored bookshop owned by Dusty Teal, an old river-ratting pal of Ed's. It was a favor typical of Abbey's generosity to friends, and the last stop, an addendum actually, to a murderous four-week, coast-to-coast promo tour for Ed's most recent novel, *The Fool's Progress.* Ed was frankly relieved to have that particular job of work behind him, swearing it was "absolutely the *last* time" he'd ever tour. (Suggesting more than I could know.)

Ed seemed to enjoy himself immensely on that final visit, elated to be back in the rural Southwest, back home. Cheery, chipper and ornery as ever.

For an instance: At a restaurant called the Ore House one evening, Ed complained to our waiter about the size of his cloth dinner napkin, pretending outrage, calling it "a damn postage stamp!" The young waiter was game, taking away the offending item and returning momentarily with a red-checkered table cloth. Not to be one-upped, Ed accepted the sheet-sized replacement with a mock-serious, deep-voiced "now *that's* more like it." Unfurling the prize, he tucked a fat corner into his shirt collar and resumed his meal. Only after the waiter had left did he break into a huge, triumphant grin.

The next day, we drove up onto a piñon-juniper mesa a few miles above town and hiked for an hour into a biting late-November wind, walking and talking the cold away. Despite the unfriendly weather, Ed insisted on a hike.

Abbey was a compulsive walker, doing a mile or two most every morning, again in the cool of evening, and finding the time for frequent days-long backpack treks. Once, just before his sixtieth birthday, equipped with an antique frame pack, aspirin and Demerol, he hiked 115 miles in six days, alone, across perhaps the truest desert wilderness North America has left. Each night's hike (he rested through the blistering mid-days) was a life-or-death race to reach another water source before the morning sun renewed its relentless assault. (Ed once suggested that the rivers of highly alkaline water he'd drunk in his long career of desert ratting might have contributed to the pancreatic hysteria and esophageal bleeding that was slowly killing him.)

Though we always walked when we got together—up and down the desert wash that meanders close behind *chez* Abbey on the west edge of Tucson, among the sandstone hobgoblins of southeast Utah, amongst the cool aspen forests surrounding my mountain cabin— I'd never gotten to join Ed on a *real* hike. During our last little stroll together above Durango, we laid plans to remedy that. There was a place, he told me, a magical desert valley. We'd go there soon ... Ed, Jack Loeffler and I would rendezvous in early March for a week of wilderness camping and hiking and companionable bull-shooting.

Sure we would.

At visit's end, Ed handed me a copy of *The Fool's Progress*, held open to an inscription scrawled large on the title page: "For my good friend Dave Petersen and his great wife Caroline—companions on this fool's journey out of the dark, through the light, into the unknown."

I knew Ed had been sick, off and on, for quite some time, but I was unaware of just *how* sick. I had no idea he was dying, nor did many others; I guess he didn't want to burden anyone unnecessarily. (Now, how I wish he'd burdened me.) But even in my ignorance, that haunting *Fool's Progress* inscription foreshadowed the dark side. Standing there with that big book in my hand, I recalled in rapid replay ...

• My first nervous meeting with Edward Abbey, famous writer and (I'd been warned) curmudgeon extraordinaire. I'd come to Tucson to conduct a magazine interview—a meeting it had taken me weeks of back-and-forth letter exchanges and uneasy telephone conversations to win.

On the appointed morning, we met on the courtyard patio of the venerable and elegant (Ed's term) Arizona Inn and talked through a sunny Sonoran January day, nursing *Cerveza Coronas* to ease the tension between mutually suspicious strangers. It worked. ("Beer for breakfast," commented my host, loosening up, "is one of the good things in life.") Our conversation ranged late into the night and was the longest and most detailed interview Ed would ever give. It was also the beginning of a friendship destined to die even as it flowered.

• The time I asked Ed if he could write an essay for a magazine I was helping to launch—it would impress my employer and gain the fledgling publication instant attention—and Ed politely, reluctantly declining, explaining that he was already swamped with writing commitments and pressured by looming deadlines. Then, a week or so later, "River Solitaire" turned up in my mailbox, accompanied by a note saying "I found this story in my journals and typed it up. It's fairly loose writing, but it's yours if you want it." Loose writing it certainly was not, and I knew that once again, Ed had taken time he didn't have in order to help a friend.

• That awkward occasion when Ed spontaneously offered to loan me a thousand dollars, no conditions, after I'd carelessly whined that times were a little hard.

• His generous mentorship, repeatedly offering to sponsor me (and other struggling writer-friends) with his agent and publishers.

• And, most vividly, I recalled the experience that had introduced me to Cactus Ed: my first reading of *Desert Solitaire*. That book, that experience, was a life-changing epiphany, opening my sleepy eyes to the heartbreaking beauty of the natural world, to the bittersweet mystery of life on this miraculous earth, our one true home. "The only home," Ed noted, "we will ever know."

❧

But now it was time for the Abbeys to leave. We shook hands, exchanged *abrazos,* said our so-longs—"*Adios, amigo;* see you in March for that desert camping trip"—then Ed folded himself into the old truck alongside his wife and children ... and was gone.

On March 4, the day before I was to leave for my spring rendezvous with Ed and Jack, complications at home forced me to phone Tucson and beg off. Graciously, Ed concurred with my excuses. "Don't worry about it, Dave; there'll always be another day."

Ten days later, Ed Abbey was dead. He was barely sixty-two.

Thinking back on that last phone conversation now, Ed was right—there *would* be another day, and this is it.

I breath deep the spicy desert air, wondering at the mysterious fragrances rising from the blackness of the valley below—the selfsame valley, ironically, that Ed had wanted to share with me three years ago. It is a place, I am learning, where phantoms come to brood and mourn.

If you go there you must hear them ... where the air is cool and sweet with the odor of juniper and lightning, where the mockingbird and the canyon wren and the mourning dove join with the phantoms in their useless keening.

Abbey country.

In blinding blackness I squat beside the crude headstone and say to Ed the things I've come all the long way here to say—then lace boot loosely over injured foot, pull on pack, stand and tip my cap to this good, wise man I was so very fortunate to have known. As a parting gesture—there's nobody here to call me maudlin—I place an expensive cigar, the kind Ed preferred but rarely indulged in, on the sand beside his headstone.

Our visit finished (for now), I turn and limp into the night, resuming my own fool's journey, into the great unknown.

10

Peacock's War

IN THE SUMMER OF 1984 I was asked by *Mother Earth News,* for whom I then labored as western editor, to attend the annual Round River Rendezvous of the so-called radical environmental group Earth First! Specifically, the magazine wanted a "Plowboy Interview" with EF! cofounder and de facto chieftain Dave Foreman (who now, in a slam-dunk of irony, sits on the board of the Sierra Club).

The EF! meet was to be held on private land along the Clark Fork River in the Yaak Valley of northwestern Montana—clearcut country, redneck heaven, a bastion of "wise use" radicalism long before the term was coined. Things could get nasty. I jumped at the chance to go.

When I mentioned the upcoming trip to my friend Edward Abbey, he told me to be sure and say hello for him to one of his oldest and closest comrades. Doug Peacock, he'd heard, had agreed to come down from his hermit's (fire-watch) tower in Glacier National Park to preach to the assembled Earth First! multitudes on the glories of grizzly bears and grizzly wilderness, his primary passions.

I knew that Peacock had been a model for the burly, red-eyed rowdy "George Washington Hayduke" in *The Monkey Wrench Gang,* Abbey's wildly comedic novel of environmental anarchy. And that was about all I knew of the man. I looked forward to meeting him and told Ed I would be sure to relay his hello.

"Just remember," said Ed in parting, "Doug is brilliant, educated, eloquent, passionate, sensitive, a fierce warrior with a heart big as a house ... but he can also be loud, brash, domineering, bull-headed and maddening as hell. He's one of the most complex people I've ever known. But I love him like a brother. And once you get to know him, so will you."

As things turned out, I never got a chance to look up Peacock in Montana; he found me first. I'd arrived the evening before, crashed for the night in a lumpy meadow under a star-spangled Big Sky firmament and had just finished a morning interview with Foreman. The day was heating up and Foreman and I were lounging in the shade under a huge old hay wagon that had been pulled into a corner of the meadow to serve as a stage, when up walked two hirsute pyknic brutes. From a distance they looked like brothers, except that one had a distinctly undulant, you could almost say ursine walk. He looked to be a handful of years older than me and spoke with a voice like a growl.

"You must be Petersen," he rumbled. "I'm Peacock. Abbey said I should look you up."

Peacock introduced his sturdy companion as Lance Olsen, president of the Montana-based Great Bear Foundation. They took seats in the grassy shade of the wagon across from Foreman and me. Then, from a soiled canvas belt-pouch big as a bible, Peacock produced a plastic flask, uncapped it and took a long pull. Smacking his lips, he thrust the bottle at me and grunted, "George Dickel and branch-water." I helped myself.

That evening, Peacock went on the wagon to deliver a sermon that was at once passionate and convincing. His topic was protecting grizzly bears and grizzly wilderness as a way of protecting the sanity and sanctity of the human race. Dave Foreman followed, unleashing an incendiary preservationist oration filled with all the fire and brimstone of a Southern Baptist tent revival (in which ambiance he was raised). Get Peacock and Foreman together on the same stage (or wagon), and you've got yourself one hallelujah of a green chautauqua.

∽

That was how I came to know Douglas "Arapaho" Peacock. Today, I'd be hard-pressed to recall what all passed between us that afternoon and night and the next morning before I had to leave that lovely, if too-much-abused, Montana place. I doubt if Doug remembers either. But we hit if off slick as deer guts on a doorstep, and our paths have crossed with an irregular frequency ever since. Being friends with Doug, as Abbey had suggested, is a four-wheel joy ride, bumpy as hell but never boring and withal, an honor. Days and nights spent with Peacock are days and nights never forgotten.

Like the June afternoon when Doug and his long-time sidekick Dan Sullivan made an unannounced stop in Durango, en route from Tucson to Glacier. Peacock phoned to say they had a few hours to kill and did I want to drive into town and meet them for a drink. I suggested Olde Tymer's, a boisterous Main Street saloon-cafe. When I arrived, half an hour later, Doug and Dan had anchored a back-corner booth and started without me. For two hours we bent elbows and jawed.

When the afternoon cooled toward evening, Peacock insisted on picking up more than his share of the bar tab, and the three of us slouched out onto the bustling streets of Durango and wobbled around the corner to where Doug had parked his truck. After growling at Dan for the keys, Doug unlocked the camper shell, reached into a big box filled with smaller boxes and came out with a fresh quart of Herradura. Thus armed, we slouched around yet another corner to the first sidewalk bench we came to—just down from the Durango Police station, as it happened—and sat there until dark talking quietly and passing the brown-bagged bottle, like the ad hoc derelicts we were.

The perplexing thing about that day was that none of us ever got properly drunk—not that we didn't give it our best shots (shot after shot). Just good clean fun, Peacock style. And quite a financial splurge for all of us.

Back then, Doug's only income of record was earned as a wilderness fire lookout during the summer months. But he wore his poverty proudly, boasting that he'd never earned enough in any year since leaving the army to necessitate filing a tax return. I too am a disciple of personal freedom via voluntary poverty, so it naturally became a game with Doug and me to compare our portfolios each time we got together. He with the highest recent annual earnings was the loser and had to buy the drinks. It's a wager I'd be sure to win against most anyone, most anytime. Except for Peacock.

Not long after that memorable semidrunk Durango afternoon, Peacock's fortunes caught an unexpected updraft when *American West* editor Tom Pew learned that Doug had a book in progress. Pew asked to see the manuscript, and following some argument, Doug reluctantly produced it. Pew scanned the sloppy, shop-worn pile of typed and scribbled-over pages and would later comment that "the writing was beautiful, and the feeling was more." When Pew asked permission to print an excerpt from the incomplete book-in-progress, Doug was edgy, saying he wasn't sure if it, or he, was ready for public exposure. But Pew persisted and a few months later ran the story "A Gathering of Grizzlies." From the opening paragraph ...

The bushes part, and a chocolate brown grizzly bear steps into the mountain clearing. Cautiously, he ambles over the downed timber swinging his huge dish-shaped head from side to side. His dark hump, the mound of muscle between his shoulders providing the source of the great swiping and digging power of the most awesome carnivore on the continent, is enormous. At five hundred pounds, when he stands, he towers a head above my own. The big bear stops. He stiffens and thrusts his nose up into the cool evening air, reaching for a scent of the intruder. He rears, his jaws agape, and slowly spins on his hind feet as if in a gentle dance. Suddenly he bolts down the mountain, through the basin, huffing and rolling over the deadfalls as easily as water cascades over rapids. His vast rippling flanks disappear as he reaches the timber.

In that same issue of *American West,* editor Pew wrote a long intro-
duction, calling Peacock's piece "one of the finest articles we've ever
published. ... In fact, Doug's whole persona—writer, Vietnam vet,
modern-day mountain man, father and born-again-as-a-white-man
Grizzly Bear—is pretty hard to match." He went on to dub the author
"Mr. Griz."

Peacock's next triumph came with the completion, in 1988, of a
project he'd been quietly plugging away at for years. The autobiographical film *Peacock's War* documents Doug's extended bloody
combat tour in Vietnam as a Green Beret medic, his return to "the
world" as a walking claymore mine and the ephiphanous healing he
experienced among the grizzlies in the wild backcountry of
Yellowstone and Glacier National Parks.

Peacock's War was aired by PBS to award-winning acclaim, prompting a vigorous demand for personal appearances. Soon, Doug found
himself thrust into a national speaking tour. While this unexpected
upturn of fortunes robbed him of coveted time with family at home
and grizzlies afield, it also provided the perfect vehicle for his crusade
on behalf of wildness.

Thus encouraged and energized, the former fire lookout got back
to work on his long-sidelined book. In 1990, *Grizzly Years: In Search
of the American Wilderness* was released by the prestigious New York
house Henry Holt and was promptly and universally hailed by critics
as a "nature writing" classic. In fact, it's a whole lot more than that ...

Something was wrong. On the outside I was calm, even passive, but
there was something frenzied on the inside. I drove nonstop for two
days at exactly forty-seven miles per hour, driving with a head full of
leftover combat-issue dextroamphetamine, partially counteracted by a
steady trickle of six-packs. Finally I found myself asleep at the wheel
in the middle of Kansas. I checked into a run-down motel, not
wanting to camp among crop-covered fields, and jumped into a hot
shower. Coming out, I flipped on the tube to the evening news. There

was the war I had just left, blaring out over the TV, the entire catastro-
phe before my eyes in black and white. Suddenly a close-up of a snow
goose appeared on the screen. "There are no easy answers." The
camera panned the swamp, revealing an oil refinery in the distance.
"... Can oil and wildlife mix?" Something snapped. I buried my fist in
the face of the smiling mustached man in the hard hat.

The next morning I bandaged my hand, paid for the television set,
and climbed back into the jeep.

On July 4, 1987, Doug and Abbey and I bivouacked for the night out
on a moonscape slickrock bench along the old dirt entrance road
(now, thanks to flagrant abuse by off-road bicyclists, gated and
locked) to Arches National Park, Utah. Ed provided the chow and
Doug grilled it to drooling perfection on a campfire of sage—then,
upholding his reputation as a culinary master—at the appropriate
moment produced a litre of the perfect wine (so far as I know). I
kicked in a case of cheap beer and some grocery store cigars for
dessert.

After dark, I sat back in humbled ignorance while Doug and Ed held
a friendly debate on pedantic particulars of the nocturnal Utah heavens. Long past midnight, I got my first dose of Mr. Griz's eccentric
habit of slipping away from camp, sleeping bag in hand, to den alone
beneath some hidden bush or tree, far beyond the firelight's glow.

"Does it all the time," Ed remarked as we watched him go. "A tick
he brought back from the war."

An indoor version of this same denning instinct was related to me
some years later by Terry Tempest Williams, first lady of southwestern literature and like a big sister to Doug (though Terry is the
younger). One fall a few years back, Terry came to town to read at the
(sadly, now-defunct) Durango Literature Conference. Doug had
been hiking in Comb Wash, just over the border in southeastern
Utah, and made the half-day drive here for a visit. As a guest of Fort
Lewis College, Terry was staying at the Strater Hotel, an elegant 19th

century Victorian. Doug, being Doug, was traveling on a bootlace and planned to sleep in his truck. The night was plenty cold, so Terry invited Doug to sneak his sleeping bag up to her room and crash on the cushy carpet.

"I love Doug," Terry told me the next day. "Instead of just rolling his bag out on the floor, he gathered up all the loose chairs in the room and stacked them in a corner to make a little cave, like we all did as kids, then crawled inside to sleep."

Peacock has many such eccentricities—many endearing, a few maddening as hell—all of which can be summed up as unpredictable. Not to be confused with unreliable. For friends in need, Peacock is rock-steady. To wit ...

On the bad night of March 13, 1989, when Ed Abbey lay dying, Doug was there to help ease the passage. Ed's end was prolonged and painful, but, says Doug, "the bravest and most dignified dying" he'd ever witnessed. And he's witnessed more than any man's fair share.

Peacock was also there, along with three other friends good and true, to bear Ed's mortal shell far into a desert wilderness for an outlaw burial in a carefully secreted redoubt offering "an Abbey kind of view."

In a letter soon after, Peacock told me of "the last night of madness" following Abbey's death and anarchist's burial: "I took the couch Ed died on out to the desert and burned it. Sat up all night in front of an ironwood fire spitting fine tequila into the flames. At daylight there was a Bowie knife stuck in the arm. [Novelist] Jim Harrison called ... and commented that the French have a phrase for the difficulty of coming back after walking a friend into death (too far into). Can't recall it just now."

❧

In 1991, Peacock brought his crusade for grizzly bears and grizzly wilderness to my own backyard, and changed my life in the doing. After personal explorations into the high backcountry of the South

San Juans had convinced him that hopeful rumors he'd been hearing were likely true, Doug founded the San Juan Grizzly Project, a (then) volunteer group dedicated to proving that a remnant population of native grizzlies still roam these increasingly tortured southern Rockies. Doug encouraged me to join the search, which I did, though remaining independent of his group. For the next several years, that quest consumed my life, as documented in the (unintentionally) underground book *Ghost Grizzlies: Does the Great Bear Still Haunt Colorado?* Thus did one little corner of Peacock's war become Petersen's war, and my life is all the richer for it.

Today, Doug is single again and holing up near Livingston, Montana, on secluded property owned by celebrity friend (just one of many) Jeff Bridges, in the movie-set whorehouse from *Heaven's Gate.* From there, Doug spent this exceptionally bad Northern Rockies winter just past hurling the full brunt of his passion and influence against the bureaucratic, self-serving forces responsible for the unconscionable and wholly unnecessary slaughter of eleven hundred Yellowstone National Park bison.

From Doug Peacock's journal-based essay "The Yellowstone Massacre" (the *Audubon* magazine cover story for May, 1997):

> [Biologist] Meagher now says that "the park herds do not face extermination" and calls the winterkill a "critical ecological need" because the Yellowstone herd had become "inflated." A coldhearted observation, perhaps true of the bison inside the park, though I sometimes wish retention of soul were a necessary piece of a doctorate in biology. ... I recall a refrain from Vietnam: "We had to destroy the village in order to save it."

A new book, *Walking It Off,* documenting Peacock's profound experiences with life and death and love and loss, is in the works.

After a decade and a half of friendship, I still can hardly think of Mr. Griz without recalling Abbey's prophetic profile: "Doug is brilliant, educated, eloquent, passionate, sensitive, a fierce warrior with a heart as big as a house ... but he can also be loud, brash, domineering, bull-headed and maddening as hell. He's one of the most complex people I've ever known. But I love him like a brother. And once you get to know him, so will you."

Ed's final novel, written at a race-horse pace during the weeks immediately preceding his death and published posthumously, is titled *Hayduke Lives!* Through Doug Peacock, he does indeed.

11

Killing Fish with the Milagro Man

I'D BEEN READING his books and admiring his landscape photo art for years, but I'd never met John Nichols, and he didn't know me from beans. But in 1989 I phoned him up to talk about our mutual friend Ed Abbey, whose recent death I was struggling to comprehend. Nichols was warm and unaffected; he even made me laugh. The next autumn, I invited John to read at the Durango Literature Conference at Fort Lewis College, where I taught part-time. He came, and proved to be as down-to-earth and charismatic in person as he is in print and on the phone.

The college auditorium was jammed with an audience of several hundred. After introductions, John stepped to the lectern and surprised us all with a pretty good Elvis imitation. He then launched into an extended reading from his most recent book, *The Sky's The Limit: A Defense of the Earth.* Mid-program, a notoriously dimwitted (now ex) professor of English seated behind me complained in a loud whisper to his wife (now ex), "I thought this was going to be about *literature.*" Afterwards, I mentioned this criticism to John; he laughed and fired back, "But environmental writing is literature!"

Through the following months, Nichols and I exchanged occasional letters and phone calls, and enjoyed an impromptu three-day visit the summer of 1991 in Wyoming.

Then, in August of 1992, Caroline flew off to California for a high school reunion. She was young and beautiful and gone. I felt old and lonesome and vaguely jealous. My salvation was a phone call from John inviting me to Taos to "kill some fish." From Durango to Taos is an easy, eye-popping half-day's drive, and I hit the road next morning.

Nichols had recently bought a dilapidated old adobe (a "Taos charmer" in real estate bullshitese) a few blocks off the plaza. I found it after some effort, hidden in plain sight in the quaint maze of Taos back streets. That evening we gorged on Rio Grande rainbow trout from John's freezer, drank good cheap beer and talked beyond midnight.

In the morning we made sandwiches and jumped into John's 1980 Dodge pickup—the biggest piece of junk you've ever seen and the only motorized vehicle he's owned for years—and went rattling out across the mesa. After several miles, we dropped off the blacktop and bumped along several more miles of dusty backroads. When the old truck finally quit rolling, we were sitting within spitting range of a thousand-foot plunge into the Rio Grande Gorge.

Peeking over the edge of that gaping gash is a glimpse into eternity, going and coming. It seemed impossible that we could ever work our way down to the sunken ribbon of river that carved through the bottom, but John knows the Gorge like a lover and led out along the rim to a safe descent. We arrived at water's edge a half-hour later, a little weak-kneed but otherwise in fine fettle, and made ready to kill us some fish.

We were hardly Orvis models, Nichols and I. Had you seen us, in fact, you'd probably have expected us to be toting cane poles and coffee cans of worms rather than fly rods. When I joked about this to John, he inspected his tattered t-shirt, stained chinos and holed tennis shoes—no waders or fishing vest—chuckled and allowed as how "fashion doesn't count for much with trout."

Anxious to get on with it, I tied on a #14 parachute Adams, a generic mayfly imitation that's always done me well in the small mountain streams of home. Before Nichols had even gotten his rod jointed together, I was flailing the nearest eddy.

Unhurried, John took a seat on a boulder, of which there are thousands in the Gorge, and affixed a #12 Charley's Killer, a wet pattern resembling a hairy black ant, custom tied by his good friend and fellow Rio Grande flymaster Charley Reynolds. He then rigged a trailing tippet a couple of feet long, to which he tied an identical Reynolds creation.

Ready at last, Nichols went hopping out across a slippery step-stone bridgework toward a ripple of shallow water. There, he unlimbered with a few false casts, cleanly uncoiling a long loop of line. After waiting a few seconds, he began a slow twitching retrieve. Suddenly his rod tip jerked sharply down, then up as he responded to the take. Surely, I thought, he's not onto a fish on the very first cast! But he was, and following a brief struggle, landed a gorgeous rainbow of about fifteen inches.

Just like that.

I watched as Nichols unhooked and returned the beautiful animal to its liquid world, then rock-hopped upstream to a fresh splash of water—and promptly landed a second, even larger fish.

And so it went. I have never seen anyone fish harder or enjoy it more than John Nichols did that glaring August day, grinning all the while. When it comes to angling, this man definitely has the *milagro* touch.

By evening, after trying every trick in my admittedly limited repertoire and every fly in my raggedy vest—plus a Reynolds Killer provided by my guide and promptly ambushed by a lurking osier—I remained skunked. I had, however, managed to fall in the river twice, rock-bashing and almost drowning my "new" 35mm SLR, which I'd only days before gotten back from the repair shop after dropping it off a Colorado cliff earlier in the summer while out searching for ghost grizzlies.

Nichols, meanwhile, had landed more than a dozen gorgeous big trout. The last two "small lunkers" (his term)—a sleek rainbow and a stocky brown, sixteen and seventeen inches respectively—John decided to keep for dinner, grimacing and apologizing to the fish even as he administered a swift *El Bonko*. The others went promptly back into the river. He talks tough, but when you get right down to it, Nichols is a decidedly reluctant fish killer.

As the sun sank beyond the yawning jaws of the Gorge, two-thirds of a mile above us, we began the long pull rimward. I knew that John had life-threatening heart problems, and pondering the climb ahead of us I couldn't help but worry (notwithstanding I was wheezing louder than he). But we took it easy, with frequent short breathers, and eventually gained the truck in good order.

There, John cracked open an ice chest, lifted out a dripping cold six-pack of good cheap beer and filled its void with the catch of the day. In no hurry to be anywhere else at all, we sat on the rusty tailgate and drank and jawed our way through a blatantly opulent sunset. When the first sixer was history, John "discovered" a second lurking beneath the fishy ice. The night was cave dark when we cruised slowly back to Taos, hungry as ospreys.

End of a good day in the Gorge, killing fish with the *Milagro* Man.

ℚ

John Treadwell Nichols was born July 23, 1940 in Berkeley, California. His mother died of heart disease when he was two (and she only twenty-seven), and across his first fourteen years he lived in Berkeley, New York, Berkeley again, Connecticut, Vermont, Virginia and D.C. From fourteen to eighteen he attended the Loomis School in Connecticut, spending his summers working as florist, farmer, lifeguard and dish washer.

In 1957, between his junior and senior years in prep school, Nichols spent a summer cruising the Southwest, paying his way by mudding an adobe house in Taos, collecting insect specimens for a biological research station in southern Arizona, fighting fires in the Chiricahua Mountains—and "subsistence fly fishing." When he returned to the East, he carried back with him a deep affection for the West and its denizens, terrestrial and aquatic, human and non.

During his final year of prep school, a prototype *Milagro Beanfield War* was already swimming around in Nichols's head. Within months of his return from New Mexico, the school-boy novelist had written a novella called "The Journey." The setting is the Southwest and the story turns on the protagonist, a young *mestizo* named Francisco, taking his blind Indian grandfather into the mountains to die:

> The climbing became steeper and more than once the horses slipped on the wet stones in the trail. Then they rounded a curve in the trail and came into a clearing on the side of the mountain. Just as they entered the clearing, the sun burst into view and Francisco exclaimed at the rainbow, which arced over the flats below. The air was clear and Francisco could see far out onto the desert. He could see the pueblos, and the town beyond. His Tata listened as Francisco described the rainbow, and the tiny specks which were the buffalo herd, and the thin curls of smoke coming from the pueblos. Francisco described to him the fields, and the little circular fingerprints on the land made by the plows. The desert country was resting in all the bright colors of autumn and there was a patchwork of the mellow browns and reds in the places where the trees were. When Francisco looked at the old man he saw that he was smiling.

Nichols graduated from Hamilton College (New York) in 1962 and spent the next year living with his grandmother in Barcelona. There he taught English at the *Instituto Norteamericano*, immersed himself in Pablo Neruda, Garcia Lorca, Juan Ramon Jimenez and other Spanish-language literary greats, all while working on his first novel.

In 1963 Nichols moved to New York City and took a cold-water flat ("forty-two bucks a month") among Italian and Puerto Rican neighbors. There he studied, became politically active and supported himself by playing guitar in coffee houses, hawking "quasi-pornographic" drawings on Greenwich Village streets, washing dishes and short-order cooking. He also wrote, working on five novels simulta-

neously. In 1964 he sold the fifth of the five, *The Sterile Cuckoo,* to the
New York publishing house David McKay for an advance of $500. He
was twenty-three years old.

That same year Nichols visited Guatemala, where he acquired a
lasting respect and empathy for the oppressed peasantry of Central
and South America. In 1969 he migrated to Taos.

There, Nichols joined local Hispanic and Indian activists in their
political and legal battles against the rampant growth that threatened
to destroy both the traditional Taos Valley culture and the fragile
ecology upon which it subsists.

It was during this time that Nichols met the characters, learned the
folkways and experienced the epiphanies that inform *The Milagro
Beanfield War.* The novel was inspired, he says, by a "radical political
dream" that common people, united, can triumph over the tyranny
of the rich and rapacious.

Published in 1974 by Holt, Rinehart and Winston, *Milagro* became
Nichols's third novel to see print (*The Wizard of Loneliness* was the
second) and "about the twentieth" he had written. *Milagro,* he recalls,
"got some nice reviews, then sank like a stone." But good news trav-
els fast, and eight months before the novel's release, *Milagro* had been
taken under option for filming. A year's-long roller-coaster ride
ensued, during which annual film options, never more than $5000,
kept Nichols in groceries.

Finally, in 1986, New Mexico documentary producer Moctesuma
Esparza, with support from the National Council of La Raza and in
partnership with Robert Redford, began filming. It was Redford's
debut as a director.

Surprisingly, considering the media attention *Milagro* received,
Nichols reports that the $15 million production was "a phenomenal
commercial and critical bust. It went way over budget. And when it
finally got released, reviews were mixed. It was given only limited
release in the U.S. and then went immediately into video, never earn-
ing back its cost. Even so, I was grateful—after all the agony, stress,

tension, fears and apprehensions—that in the end it was a decent little film with dignity and political and cultural integrity, a film that broke the negative Hollywood stereotypes of Mexican culture."

Nichols adds that the making of *Milagro* was "an agonizing process fraught with apprehensions. In the end, boy was I grateful it was over. And there was never much of what people identify as 'success' concerned with it. My lifestyle didn't change, except that I lost my anonymity and privacy for a year and everybody *thought* I must be a stinking billionaire because Redford was connected with the project. Fact is, the film cost me a fortune picking up checks, returning phone calls and buying tickets for everybody I knew in New Mexico to go to the two benefit openings. I kept using the same outhouse the whole time, driving the same truck I drive today and giving away any excess bread that came along. Ultimately, what I got out of that experience was a greatly exacerbated heart condition."

Since then, Nichols has continued to work "fairly steadily" in films and earns "a good living," though he shuns anything approaching a materialistic lifestyle. He continues to live simply, has helped put several "kids," his own and others, through college and gives generously to the many causes he supports. Celebrity, he says, has never interested him. It's a claim his lifestyle confirms.

ॐ

On my most recent visit with the *Milagro* Man—it was a wintry fall day, too blustery and miserable to fish—we spent an afternoon and evening hiking the steep hills surrounding Taos, then returned to the Nichols' adobe for dinner. Afterward, John played guitar, his lovely and talented wife Miel danced flaminco and we drank and talked.

Late in the evening, my host produced a paperback copy of the letters of Gustave Flaubert, paged through the tattered volume for a moment, found what he was looking for and read aloud a section in which Flaubert laments to a friend that it has taken him six weeks of intense writing and revising to produce just thirteen polished pages of a novella he was thinking of calling *Madame Bovary.*

John tossed the book on the kitchen table with a thump. "How I'd love to be able to achieve that depth of artistic perfection in my writing."

I thought about that, about *Madame* and *Milagro,* about which I prefer and why. "In art," I heard myself saying, "results count more than effort."

When I looked at John Nichols, I saw that he was smiling.

PART FOUR

❧

Out There

12

A Wilderness of Superstition

IN ONE LONG DAY, friend, ace photographer and long-time back-country companion Branson Reynolds and I have rolled back the seasons two full months—from a wintry November morning with a fresh foot of snow on the ground and seven degrees shivering on the thermometer outside our neighboring Colorado cabins, to a balmy Sonoran Desert evening. To work this seasonal sorcery, we had merely to drive ten hours south, in the process shucking off five hundred miles of latitude and five thousand feet of elevation.

Which brings us, happily, to the southern flank of the Superstition Mountains, a weirdly eroded volcanic moonscape in south-central Arizona's upper Sonoran Desert.

The Sonoran is no glaring, get-across-it-fast-as-you-can desert, like some, but mountainous and green with saguaro, ocotillo, cholla, hedgehog, barrel, prickly pear … God's (or perhaps the Devil's) own cactus garden. And thriving amongst all this thorny verdure is a cornucopia of wildlife: hawks, falcons, eagles, owls and more songbirds than you could count with an abacus; deer, javelina, coyotes, cougars, coatis, badgers and many another charismatic character.

East of Apache Junction, I swerve off the blacktop and onto a pretty good dirt road leading northeast into the mountains. "Wild looking country," observes Branson, man of few words.

Our topo map seconds that opinion through a litany of place names with their guts still in: Apache Gap, Geronimo Head, Hell's Hole, Rattlesnake Spring, Gunsight Gap, Lion Spring, Wildcat Creek, Buzzard's Roost, *Malapais* (Evil Place) Mountain, Devil's Canyon, Haunted Canyon.

As we bounce along, a red-tailed hawk shadows us from above, perhaps having learned that moving vehicles often scare up roadside rodents. Only after several minutes does the gorgeous bird lose interest and glide away.

Before long, our pretty good road gives way to a hillside goat trail, the essence of steep, narrow, rutted and rocky. I shift into four-by/low and we grind slowly upward, inching ever closer to the trailhead gateway to a long down-canyon hike in search of a little-known prehistoric Indian cliff dwelling. (And so far as I'm concerned, it should stay little-known; to hell with guidebooks to unspoiled places and the perpetrators thereof.)

In selecting this hike from the 250 miles of trails warping through the 159,780-acre Superstition Wilderness, our first goal was privacy. The trail down through our chosen canyon, I've been assured, is rarely used, faint at best and in places entirely washed out. Good. And since we'll be hiking midweek, our desert solitude is virtually guaranteed. What's more, this being winter, pothole and spring water should be plentiful.

Had we elected to hike on a better-known trail with easier access, our Superstitions experience would be shockingly different. Take, for an extreme instance, the Peralta trail. There, on any pleasant weekend, you can expect to meet swarms of fellow nature lovers, most of them day-hiking the four-mile round-tripper to Fremont Saddle. The draw is that Fremont Saddle offers a superb overview of Weaver's Needle, a volcanic plug rising fifteen hundred feet above the Superstition badlands and a fountainhead of historical mythology.

Back in 1891, a dying and delirious prospector—Jacob Waltz, "the Dutchman"—identified Weaver's Needle as the primary landmark-clue to the whereabouts of a secret gold mine. It is said that across thirty years, Waltz cashed in at least twenty grand in gold nuggets he claimed to have dug from the mine. Some reports put the figure much higher. But even twenty grand was a fistful of dollars back then. And certainly, the nuggets had to have come from somewhere, lending some credence to the hidden, or "lost" mine story.

Hitch is, the geologic probability of finding a paying gold vein in the igneous ambiance of an ancient volcanic area such as the Superstitions is ... well, zilch.

In any event, the legend of the Lost Dutchman's Mine is the most famous of Arizona's many Old West lost-treasure myths and, consequently, a tourist magnet. While only a handful of true believers actually go treasure hunting, thousands of visitors a year are curious enough to want a peek at Weaver's Needle and the hobgoblin desert terrain surrounding it. Thus the wild popularity of the Peralta trail.

Nor is the Dutchman's influence limited to spotty overcrowding. It is said that since the legend's advent in 1891, nearly seventy people have died or gone permanently missing in the Superstitions, and there are whispers of a "Dutchman's curse." It's not uncommon to encounter truculent treasure hunters armed like Pancho Villa—big kids acting out their *Treasure of Sierra Madre* fantasies. Paranoia floats like smoke on the shimmering summer heat.

Up in the mountains ahead, beyond the end of this bone-bruising road and far from Weaver's Needle, Branson and I shouldn't be bothered by any such silliness. Nor by the persistent smog—a gift from nearby Phoenix—that taints the western flanks of the Superstitions, seriously tarnishing the wilderness experience.

Still lugging in compound low, we climb above the cactus zone and into a chaparral environment dominated by brush and brushy trees—green-barked paloverde, red-skinned manzanita, mesquite, creosote, jojoba and others I can't yet put a name to.

When finally we reach the trailhead, we climb out of the truck, stretch, buckle into our packs and scurry off, racing dark, determined to enjoy a secluded trailside camp this first night out. The walking is liniment for our truck-cramped muscles and minds, but just half an hour along, having come upon a spot too appealing to bypass, we call it quits for the day.

On the jagged western horizon, down Phoenix way, a dying sun scowls angrily through a red-orange miasma of toxic haze.

Turning my back on that gaudy horror show, I select a sleeping place, fling away the largest of the rocks, spread ground cloth, inflate sleeping pad and unroll fartsack. I'm lugging a tent, but have no plans to erect it short of a meteorological emergency. Since we've elected to make this hike without a stove or any food or beverage that requires heating, I dine on canned chicken, fruit, cheese, crackers and water, then go to help Branson gather firewood.

Getting in wood in the Sonoran can be an exciting chore, given that the selfsame clump of dead brush you covet for kindling may shelter any of several species of rattlers (graceful sidewinder, Mojave ringtail, timid tiger, belligerent blacktail, deadly diamond-back), black widow or brown recluse spider, scorpion, Walapai tiger kissing bug or other cuddly local fauna. But we survive, and soon have a modest blaze crackling in a shallow pit scooped into the sandy soil.

Darkness comes and all is right—shirt-sleeve weather, a bright aromatic campfire overpowering the moonless night, a flask of amber hooch, Ursa Major turning lazily in the northern sky, crickets cricking. The only ingredients missing from this classic cowboy movie scene, Branson points out, are the questioning hoots of owls and the maniacal yodeling of coyotes. "We'll hear both before the night's out," I venture to predict.

But we don't. Instead, we hear only wind. At first just a cool breeze on the backs of our necks, in less than an hour it's howling like some satanic choir. We tire quickly of this buffeting annoyance, bank the sparking fire with sand and retreat to our body bags, sheltered slightly by thick brush all around. Before sliding in, I roll away the stone I placed on my bag as an anchor when the wind first came up, then remove and fold my jeans and jacket and cram them into my dirty t-shirt. This makes a passable pillow, into which I bury my hairy face to hide it from the gritty blow.

Desert winds I have known: the Santa Anas, roaring torch-hot down from the east, fanning conflagrations that often blacken southern California ... the schizophrenic "Devil's wind" of *Baja del Norte*, which one January night, 1980, snatched my unstaked K-Mart tent from the beach and sailed it like a box kite out into the frothing Sea of Cortez, and which might have dragged me along for the ride had I not bailed out, butt-naked, the moment my "shelter" inflated and began to shake.

By comparison, this Superstition wind is more mesmerizing than threatening, howling me soon into the dreamless sleep of the grateful dead. Or as close to it as I care to come at this stage in life.

Hours later, my bladder nags me awake. The wind blows undiminished. The stars still shine. The new moon doesn't. I worm up and out and stand—facing downwind, feet spread wide to anchor my flopping bed—and relieve the infernal pressure. It's easy to imagine my stream staying airborne for miles, a yellow mist blown all the way down to Phoenix. God knows they need the water.

Branson is up and humming well before dawn, camera in hand, hoping to capture those precious few minutes of pastel morning light that can soften even such a harsh landscape as this. But rebutting the night's gale, an ugly smog still shrouds the western horizon. And in the east, high thin clouds have appeared. "The light sucks," says Branson. True. But the wind has blessedly subsided to sporadic gusts.

I dress and breakfast on muffins and water, packing even as I eat. This will be a high-mileage day, and we're both anxious to get on with it.

We've not been walking long when we drop down into the sheltered refuge of the canyon, leaving the wind above and behind us. Soon we come upon a spring-fed *tinaja*, or pothole, carved by erosion into the gray lava rock of the creek bed. I slip free of my pack, extract water bottles and filter and move down poolside. Seemingly oblivious to my presence, a neon-blue dragonfly helicopters low over the pearlescent water, patrolling for brunch. Just below the surface, a big black beetle

sculls in slow circles, feeding lazily. One translucent *Gammarus* (scud)
scurries across the pool's sandy bottom, darting in and out of an
aquatic jungle of algae, searching frantically for ... what?

On the rock just above the pothole, Branson spots a sun-bleached,
rodent-gnawed rib bone. Largish, mammalian, we ponder its origins
... mule deer? ... prospector's burro? ... or the prospector himself
perhaps, another victim of the Dutchman's curse?

Onward.

In spring and early summer, this place would be redolent with
wildflowers—globemallow, bluedick, desert marigold and a zillion
(almost) others. Now, I spot only a scattered few—of the same three
tenacious species, in fact, that lost the seasonal fight only a month ago
back home in the high San Juans: scarlet gilia, Indian paintbrush, purple aster. In spite of the high scree of clouds, the sunlight is intense
and glaring, flattening what little color remains in the dying flowers.

Far above us, high on the steep canyon sides, the tough woody
masts of century plants rise like flagpoles above the chaparral.
Spanish bayonet and agave jab at our legs as we weave and dodge
along the narrow trail. Thorny mesquite snatches our caps, rips our
shirts and wantonly bloodies the flesh of our limbs. Shorts-and-san-
dals country this is not.

Life, and signs of life, are ubiquitous. A young cottontail bursts
from cover at my feet, squirts along the trail a ways and darts back
into the brush. Every few hundred yards, the path is marked with a
cairn of coyote or raccoon scat shot through with half-digested red
manzanita berries and jojoba nuts like slender acorns. From somewhere far above, an anonymous phainopepla bleats out its lonesome
desert anthem.

At one point, we come upon a most unusual tree. The huge
ancient specimen looks like a hardwood, but has evergreen needles
rather than leaves. Its bark is thick, pulpy and segmented into thousands of irregular rectangles. I'm perfectly baffled. But Branson, man
of quiet wisdom, identifies it as an alligator juniper. Just right.

Come mid-afternoon, with more than a few miles under our
boots, we stop to eat and reconnoiter. In my haste to get off my burning feet, I almost plop down hard on a rusty old horseshoe with the
nails still in and facing up. "Good luck," says Branson, kicking it away
just in time, then picking it up and handing it to me like a gift.

"Maybe not so lucky," I observe, "for the horse that lost it."

Certainly, we could use some luck just now. The trail has been
more off than on for the past hour and more, leaving us to fight our
way through the chaparral and repeatedly criss-cross the rocky creek
bottom. I inspect the map, hoping we haven't already missed the
ruins. "Doesn't seem possible," says Branson, and I agree. Still ...

After a feast of dried fruit, hot-pepper buffalo jerky and tepid
water, we opt to give our packs a rest and explore unburdened on
down the narrowing, increasingly rugged canyon.

We've gone less than a mile, squeezing through a neck and round-
ing a bend, when my eagle-eyed companion spots his prey. "Ruins,"
he says. I squint and strain, finally making out an adobe-colored wall
camouflaged perfectly with the buff cliff to which it clings. From
maybe thirty feet above the wall stares the dark eye of a cave.

We hurry on.

From the base of the near-vertical cliff, composed of fantastically
eroded volcanic conglomerate, we can make out two caves. The wide
mouth of the lower, smaller alcove is closed off by the crumbling wall
Branson spotted. The contents of the upper cave, if any, are invisible
from down here. We scramble up to inspect the wall.

While similarities exist between this ruin, built by the mysterious
Salado Indians about seven centuries ago, and those of the even more
ancient Anasazi—at Mesa Verde, Chaco and unnumbered elsewheres
throughout the Four Corners region—important differences are
apparent. For one, this wall has a low rectangular doorway, while your
typical Anasazi entrance is (frequently, though not always) keyhole
shaped. And while Anasazi stonemasons painstakingly shaped and fit
rectangular sandstone blocks, using adobe only to cement the blocks

together, this Salado wall is almost pure adobe, with unworked rocks of every size and shape jammed in helter-skelter as filler.

Being careful not to touch the cancerous wall—in one place, only a thin column of rotted adobe supports it—I poke my head and shoulders through the doorway. There's barely enough room inside the shallow alcove for two intimate friends to stretch out side-by. Even so, the sloping ceiling is smoke-blackened, suggesting that the tiny cell was once inhabited.

A couple of even smaller rooms, storage bins probably, and that's about it for the lower level. Anxious to explore the black-eyed cave above, we work along the cliff to where we can pick our way up.

What we find is easily worth the modest climb. This is a proper alcove cave, perhaps thirty feet across at its mouth, nearly that high and twice as deep. Several smaller chambers branching off the main room have been walled-in as sleeping and storage cells. And what we've come all the long way here to admire occupies the prime location, in the fresh air and light of the front of the cave—an almost mint-condition adobe apartment. Even the roof of the structure is largely intact, a state of preservation almost unheard of in Anasazi ruins. To look at it, you'd think its residents left only months ago.

Boxing in the front of the apartment like a courtyard fence are the roofless walls of a sister room, maybe five feet high with a single low doorway. I bend through and in, then bend again to join Branson inside the dusky apartment. The room measures maybe twelve by fourteen feet—about the size of my own little cabin's living room— with a seven-foot ceiling. The door opening is supported by lintels of sycamore the diameter of a body-builder's biceps. And in the exact center of the room, just like at home, stands a vertical roof-support post, also of sycamore.

Why, we wonder aloud, might these Neolithic people have complicated what must already have been a damn tough life by choosing to live in such a remote and inconvenient place as this, where food, water, building materials and firewood had to be lugged up or lowered down from above, and where no sizable patch of arable land is readily available?

As with the Anasazi hundreds of miles to the north, the need, real or imagined, for protection from bad guys likely provided some of the motivation. And too, they must have had a love for solitude and beauty. Bolstering the latter theory, the view from here is most agreeable; standing in the cave's yawning mouth, your gaze falls to a green-rimmed spring pool sparkling in the canyon bottom and surrounded by a jungle of brush and trees just beginning to blush with the subdued colors of a Sonoran autumn.

And how might this little clan, this extended family, have earned a living?

They would have hunted just about anything that moved and gathered wild edibles, certainly. They may also have cultivated tiny garden plots here and there. But in largest part, it is believed, the Salado earned their groceries by trading with their Hohokam relatives and neighbors, farmers who tended irrigated fields down in the bright desert valley now darkened by the rising smog-ash of Phoenix. Artifacts show the Salado to have been skilled loomers of cotton cloth and deft weavers of plant-fiber baskets, sandals and mats. But most notably, they were potters, firing elegant polychrome utensils and figurines.

Nor was this little clan alone in its chosen lifestyle. For at least two centuries, roughly 1250 to 1450 A.D., the Salado thrived in scores of similar redoubts, large and small, scattered throughout the Salt and Tonto river drainages of south-central Arizona. And then, mysteriously, the Salado, Hohokam and other prehistoric Sonoran Desert civilizations ... vanished.

Squatting now in the ancient dust of the little ruin, Branson and I fall to pondering the mental health of the cretins who have defaced this fragile shrine. One genius has tried to hack through the roof support post with a knife. And virtually every exposed wooden member has been sullied with the excrement of menial minds— carved dates ranging from 1922 to 1985, initials, even complete names: "Billy Contrares," you insignificant moron.

After a while, we bend back out and into the soft afternoon light of the open cave, having touched nothing.

Like traditional adobe structures throughout the Southwest, the roof of this apartment—one corner of which is beginning to crumble, exposing its guts to inspection—is supported by log beams set at irregular intervals, their stone-ax-hewn tips protruding through the upper walls. Atop and at right angles to the beams is laid a lattice of the tough woody ribs of saguaro cacti. And above those a tight thatch of reeds paved over with adobe clay. The result is a strong, perfectly flat patio roof suitable for work, play, cooking, dining, lovemaking and (afterwards, on warm summer nights) sleeping.

While I inspect the structure from all angles, careful not to climb upon or otherwise insult it, Branson follows with his camera, documenting every detail for his photographic memory bank. And just as well, for we may never again have an opportunity to return to this place of dusty spirits.

Sadly, even now, the time has come for us to leave.

As we skid down the cliff, then huff back up-canyon to our packs, we debate our options for tonight. Hiking down this morning, we noted that long sections of creek bank had been washed out, with clumps of plant debris deposited shoulder-high in the riparian trees and bushes—flash flood.

Something to think about.

By the time we reach our backpacks, we've grudgingly admitted that the only sane option—given the gathering gloom above us and the obvious flood-proneness of this narrow canyon—is to hike all the way back up and out before making camp. We could, of course, return to the ruins with our packs and camp there—high, safe and dry. But that strikes us both as wrong. And besides, should the canyon flood, we could be stranded for days, or have to pack umpteen unwanted bushwhack miles down, around, then back up to the truck.

I change into fresh socks and we move out.

The return hike, though uphill all the way, is not devoid of pleasures. Once, we stumble into a covey of plumed Gambel's quail, the fat little beauties exploding into flight with a cacophony of shrill cackles. And farther along, we're serenaded by the cheery, down-scale solo of a canyon wren—among the most delicate and perfect sounds in nature. Never mind the swarming gnats and skunky stench that dog us much of the way.

With evening creeping in and the fatigue of a long hiking day aching in our feet, we finally emerge from the canyon and plop down for a breather at the first level spot we come to. As we sit wiping sweat from our grimy faces and necks, a male vermilion flycatcher, its sparrow-sized body drenched in scarlet, flashes low across in front of us. A fortunate sighting. Given the lateness of the day, I become conveniently superstitious and suggest to Branson that perhaps the appearance of the fiery bird is an omen, a sign that we should camp for the night in the selfsame little clearing where we now sit. Always amiable, my good old friend grins and nods his assent.

Racing dark, as usual, we stride through the familiar rituals of gathering fuel, kindling a fire, making our beds beneath the stars. This night, unfortunately, the stars are hidden by a leaden curtain of clouds. I erect the tent and stow my pack inside, just in case.

After downing our cold dinners, we finish off the flask of firewater—why lug it any farther?—and ponder our future here. If the weather doesn't go too sour, we decide, we'll hike out to the truck in the morning, bump back down the mountain into the Sonoran life zone—where the evening air is perfumed with a spicy tang found nowhere else on earth (so far as I know)—and spend the next couple of days hiking and exploring amongst the great saguaros.

Thus, in less than a week, we will not only have rolled back the seasons to more temperate times, we'll have sampled some of the best of the two magical worlds—chaparral highlands and big-cactus desert—this spectacular "suburban" wilderness has to offer.

∽

Deep in the inky heart of the moonless night, I'm awakened by a fine mist of raindrops falling cool as stardust on my face. From somewhere nearby, two owls exchange cautious greetings ...

Who, who ... who you?

Who, who ... who, me?

In my dreamy somnolence, I imagine these phantom voices to be no mere owls, but the moaning restless spirits of Salado and Hohokam, Apache and Dutchman, destined forever to haunt this enchanted desert place. This wilderness of Superstition.

13

Baboquivari!

BABOQUIVARI! The very name is like a dream; a hard place to get
to—jeeps might do it but will be unwelcome; best come on horseback
or like Christ astride a donkey—way past the end of the pavement,
beyond the farthest smallest sleepiest town, beyond the barbed wire
(invented, some say, by a Carmelite nun), beyond the Papagoan
hogans, beyond the last of the windmills, hoving always in the
direction of the beautiful mountain.
　　　　　　—from the journals of Edward Abbey, November 1954

ONCE UPON A TIME I was granted the bittersweet honor of editing my late friend Edward Abbey's twenty-one volumes of personal journals for publication (*Confessions of a Barbarian*, 1994). Sadly, I had to leave out more than I could fit in. One of the unpublished episodes has haunted me ever since. It's a detailed, exuberantly romantic fantasy of freedom, dignity and place.

A desert place, naturally, anchored by a little island mountain range floating in the prickly midst of the Sonoran Desert southwest of Tucson. Its name is Baboquivari. Westward spreads the sparsely inhabited 2.3-million-acre Tohono O'odham (Papago) Indian Reservation. Immediately east sprawls the Altar Valley and the 120,000-acre Buenos Aires National Wildlife Refuge. To the south lie Old Mexico and the azure Sea of Cortez.

At the time of his Baboquivari journal scratchings, Abbey was a lonesome intellectual of twenty-four years, living in a dank loft in

Edinburgh, studying philosophy and literature as a Fulbright Fellow, writing his first novel ... and building desert sand castles in the air.

Baboquivari—there, somewhere, in that vast desert wasteland, I shall build my festung, *retreat, hideout ... dark womb of the soul—a long low dark sprawling sunbaked stormlashed hacienda of adobe ... a fat library of esoteric books, an arsenal of music ... all in one long open room crawling with centipedes, arachnids, vinegaroons.*

Years later, Ed would settle on (and for) the west edge of Tucson, almost within sight of Baboquivari Peak, which he visited often and climbed repeatedly. Rising nearly 4500 feet (to 7730 feet ASL) above the desert basins that surround it, Babo's bulbous granite dome offers the only class-six climb in Arizona.

Now Ed is gone, leaving me haunted by that hulking visage. Each March, to hasten the arrival of spring and honor the memory of a friend, Caroline and I flee our snowbound Colorado cabin and point ourselves southwest. This time, our destination is Baboquivari.

ॐ

BABOQUIVARI! How this name strikes on the romantic heart.

Quite so. Yet it's a name without a language, the final twisted link in a chain of awkward translations from Indian to Spanish to English. The source word, from the tongue of the indigenous Tohono O'odham—the aptly self-named "Desert People"—is *Waw* (say "vav") *Kiwulik,* or "rock drawn in at the middle."

To the O'odham, Baboquivari is holy ground. As detailed by Arizona ethnobiologist Gary Nabhan in his splendid Sonoran study *The Desert Smells Like Rain,* the Baboquivaris shelter a cave that "is *I'itoi Ki:* the home of the Coyote-like character responsible for the Papago emergence into this world. ... Because Baboquivari Peak towering over the cave can be seen from nearly every village on the reservation, this place is literally and figuratively at the heart of the Papago universe."

Today, but half of the north-south trending Baboquivaris lie within the O'odham preserve. The boundary traces the ridgeline, with the western slope belonging to the Indians and the eastern slope a checkerboard of private and public parcels. And any way you come at it, access to Baboquivari is a challenge.

You can, if you must, purchase a permit to enter tribal lands and climb Baboquivari from the west, as Abbey did on his initial attempt a quarter of a century ago (as documented in *Cactus Country*). But the O'odham are a private people and less than eager to have swarms of outsiders buzzing over their land and sacred shrines, and I don't blame them.

Fortunately, there exists a little-known route to the flanks of Baboquivari from the east, which Caroline and I snooped out and even now are exploring.

Oh my beloved Baboquivari ... here the bullbat will resound at night, the greathorned owl hunch on its haunches in the dusk, the coyote yodel wanly on the hill, the mockingbird cry and the thrush hush all; and all about, the cactus.

Cactus? Not so much, as it turns out. Westward, you bet. But here in the Altar Valley to the east of the Babos the elevation is just high enough to exclude the spectacular Sonoran cactus garden ecology in favor of an unlikely desert grassland—cow country, pard. You'll see some cholla, plenty of prickly pear, an occasional barrel, a forlorn saguaro or two, little more.

Incredibly, the drive in from the blacktop is *just* as the young Cactus Ed imagined it—*way past the end of the pavement ... over hard, dry, rocky hills on a dim trail ... under a harsh blue sky and a brilliant brassy sun ... beyond the last of the windmills, up an old dry arroyo bed paved with stone and quiet colors ... hoving always in the direction of the beautiful mountain.*

Dust-caked and butt-sore, we come at last to road's end and park the old beater in what passes for shade. After eating fresh Arizona oranges and tanking up on water, we hang packs on backs, stroll through an unlocked people portal beside the larger locked gate and follow the rocky lane to a well-kept old ranch complex—house, out-buildings, corral. The house easily predates Abbey's Babo fantasies and (as I'll bet he himself thought when first he saw it) fills his hide-out bill just so.

There it is—silent, dark, empty-seeming now, almost hidden under the trees in the lee of the red cliff, its dust-colored walls, black eyeless windows—quiet, aware, motionless, waiting.

Two big beautiful horses eye us suspiciously as we stroll boldly through their domain. Nobody else at home.

Just past the ranch complex, a trail lines out along the dry gulch of Thomas Canyon, and we lean into its moderate uphill grade. Only nine o'clock on a mid-March morning but already a "brilliant brassy sun" sizzles like napalm on exposed skin. Soon enough, though, we come beneath big, shade-making trees—mostly evergreen oaks including especially Emory and the rare Mexican blue—with the odd walnut and spindly Mexican piñon pine tossed in for variety. So many trees that at the first crossing of the gulch we lose the faint trail beneath an ankle-deep litter of leaves. With semi-method we cast about, working up-canyon, relocate the way, move along.

In contrast to the cow-burnt *plana* of the valley below—where we camped last night and saw no wildlife of any kind, though one lonely coyote did "yodel wanly" from afar—the shaded riparian corridor of Thomas Canyon offers an abundance of food, cover, even water (at least here in the lower canyon) in modest pools ringed with cattails and what I call "piss willows" in honor of their distinctly uric aroma. Wildlife abounds.

Already we've seen ground squirrels, rabbits, lizards, some big unfamiliar rodent, and we've noted evidence of others—javelina-sized bites out of prickly pear pads, coyote scats and tracks in the dust, the hard brown pellet droppings of deer. Although he mused in his journals that *at times perhaps we'll live on the dry desert air, eating sunlight and drinking the miraculous blue,* Abbey and his little society of hermits would have had no trouble keeping themselves in wild meat hereabouts.

We cross the gulch a second time, alert lest we trod upon any of the Sonoran's plethora of poisonous residents. When Caroline spots a swarm of Apoidea buzzing angrily around a head-high hole in a big live oak alongside the trail ahead—having been forewarned that Sonoran bees are "Africanized" we detour wide around. The bemused buzzers ignore us.

The higher we climb, the birdier it gets—a veritable "feathered landscape" (Terry Tempest Williams, poet). When a nervous covey of Gambel's quail scurries past just ahead, we fall into a traveling game of Name that Bird.

Most vocal and visible are the big, heavy-beaked Mexican jays, artful amalgams of raven and jay that thrive on the abundant mast in this nutty place. And twice we're blessed with flash-by glimpses of flame-red, sparrow-sized male vermilion flycatchers, among the most gorgeous of desert songsters. We hear more often than see the shy phainopeplas—big lean members of the flycatcher clan who's menfolk are glossy black with tuxedo tails and proudly crested heads. Look for phainos perched atop tall, isolated trees or cacti issuing their distinct single-note call: the Sonoran Desert anthem.

And so on—woodpeckers peck, thrashers thrash, flickers flick—at least until a pair of Harris hawks, resplendent and distinct with white-banded tails and chestnut wing and body markings, come shadowing low across the canyon, silencing and scattering the timid singers.

Far above the hawks, a swarm of swallows swirls gracefully on a right smart breeze eddying around Baboquivari massif. And hanging long and white from ledges and alcoves high on that stony visage, chalky stains like old men's beards mark the aeries of not just hawks, but eagles, ravens, even (we can suppose) that rare lovely falcon called *caracara*—the so-called "Mexican eagle" emblematic of that Nearby Faraway.

With the arrival of the hawks and the hushing of the songbirds, a liquid stillness floods the canyon. We stop and listen but hear only our own deep breathing. I look up—past trees and hawks and swallows and peak, into a flawless firmament. We've been roaming Baboland for days now, and are yet to hear or see a single stinkin' airplane.

One fat fly buzzes by, dissolving our pleasant trance. We hitch up our packs and carry on.

Our goal is a prominent notch in the ridge on the north shoulder of Baboquivari—the "drawn in at the middle" bit of O'odham fame, it would seem—where (we've been told) waits a cool, shaded, breezy campsite with a view. But no water. That must be humped all the long way up, providing this place with a built-in safeguard against overuse.

Gazing up from the ranch, the saddle didn't appear so very far, but we've been slogging for more than two hours now without a serious (sit-down) break and our goal appears not one slog closer. I've encountered this curious visual phenomenon before in the Sonoran, and lay it to the mirage-making qualities of desert light and landscape.

The trail grows increasingly steep, rocky and switchbacked as it ascends. Yet it's no worse than some "maintained" national forest trails I've hiked in the Rockies and Sierras, better than many and a lot less crowded (like, nobody).

We pass spear-leafed yucca by the dozens—Arizona and soaptree varieties, I presume—their erect penile flower stalks probing like flagstaffs at an unflawed sky. Grasses and forbs abound, though this is a lame spring for wildflowers—the winter was dry even by parched local standards—and Caroline is disappointed to spot only the odd clump of sand verbena, a few droopy stalks of sad red penstemon, a rare yellow cluster of wilted bloomers atop fish-hook barrel cactus.

The barrels, in conspiracy with mesquite, cholla, yucca, Engelmann and purple prickly pear, reach out to grab, stab and slash at our legs, making us glad we eschewed shorts in favor of pants. Alligator junipers have begun popping up among the hardwoods and piñons, growing bigger and more plentiful as we climb.

Off to our right now looms a deeply eroded rhyolite dike—a crumbling volcanic castle wall—gray-yellow rock stained lime green with lichens. To our left, lichens likewise beard the stony face of Old Man Baboquivari, enlivening his otherwise stark facade.

Noon approaches and we begin to droop. Already we've chugged a quart of water each and are wondering if we've brought enough. Moods are sinking when a tiny canyon wren flits by, gushing a joyful contrarian cascade of silvery notes that animate the arid atmosphere and revive our sagging spirits. How I love that little bird.

Directly above, a lone so-called white-throated raven (in fact merely gray-breasted) fights headlong into an invisible wind, muttering irritably to himself.

While I'm watching this spectacle in the sky, rather than the trail at my feet, a marble-sized stone shoots from beneath a clumsy boot and I go down hard, struggle to my feet (muttering irritably to myself), continue on.

And on.

Finally, after half a day of hiking, we mount Baboquivari's hirsute shoulder. I suppose an athletic young jock (or jockette), toting only the minimum of food and water and with a bee under his (or her) Bula cap, could make this hike—maybe four miles and three thousand vertical feet—in half the time. Good on him (or her). While it's no marathon, neither is it any cake walk and we've done well enough, Caroline and I. Perhaps too well. I mean—why rush it? Like life itself, rare is the destination that justifies a harried journey.

The saddle fulfills its promise—breezy and cool and deeply shaded. Plenty of room for two or even three small tents on fairly level packed earth. Long used (for millennia, no doubt), but little littered (a miracle these trashy days). A few minutes of local hunting and gathering should net plenty enough down-and-dead wood for a small evening conflagration. From here it's (mine to hope) an easy hike to the base of the mighty dome—should I decide, come morning, to attempt those last potentially killer thirteen-hundred-plus vertical feet.

This place is, in fact, the ideal approach camp for anyone planning to attack the peak from the east: a relaxed half-day up here, rest and enjoy ... a full day to do the dome and return before dark ... out the third day and (sigh) back to the "real" world.

Peering east from this vantage, you can see a hundred miles (it seems), out across the beef-bashed Altar Valley to the Coronado National Forest (likewise overgrazed and, consequently, mesquite infested). Seven distinct island ranges ring the Altar (they say), though you'd be hard pressed to separate and name them, even from such a fine observatory as this.

Feeling light as angels without our packs, we float on up the trail above the campsite, looking for a window through the trees from which to spy out the O'odham world lying westward and below. No such luck (can't see the desert for the trees). What we can see, however, is wild and rewarding—except, perhaps, for Kitt Peak at the northern terminus of the range, upon whose bald pate are visible two of the squadron of observatory domes perched there, glowing white and round like the eggs of reptilian invaders from Mars.

Directly below us rises yet another jagged broken castle wall of lichen-greened rhyolite. Beyond that and far, far below, a few patches of Indian Country come winking through, bearded over with some three hundred species of cacti. Down there, somewhere, hides old *I'itoi,* the O'odham god—who must be sleeping, since down there also, his six thousand Desert People are in pain. They still have their homeland, much of it, but like so very many indigenous peoples worldwide, they've lost their spiritual roots and, consequently, their health, perhaps their very souls.

A tangerine twilight stirs intermittent breezes, and what few bugs there were today—flies, gnats, killer bees—disappear with the sun. Sitting here staring into the winking flames of our little fire, my cholesterol-clogged old heart skips a beat with the thought that a reliable sighting of an errant Mexican jaguar—a *jaguar*—was made in Brown Canyon, *just* south of here, *just* last week. Not even the romantic young Abbey envisioned such a miracle.

The flames flicker and fade to coals, the coals wink out and the night grows suddenly chill and dark, our only light a wan yellow rocker of quarter-moon.

The desert moon—there is magic for you ... a bridge of ghostlight from here through space to the other world ... a lonely moon above a lonely land.

A lonely land, indeed. And hauntingly quiet. Even the owls, coyotes and poor-wills are mute this idyllic spring night.

∞

Morning.

Before abandoning this long-sought place—which, like so many cherished others, I may never see again (how are we to know?)—I opt to explore farther up the trail as it approaches and spirals westward around the skyscraping vertical dome. Caroline, sensible as always, elects to stay in camp "to go for help if you don't come back." I've been cautioned against attempting the ascent alone, even the relatively "easy" class-four route. (The hard bit, as always, is getting back down.) But I'm carrying a fifty-foot length of stout nylon rope and I've got all day and a heartful of energy. We'll see.

And see we do, straight-away, when I hit serious snow, freezing me out, as it were, almost before I begin. On the hike up yesterday we spotted a few scattered patches of anomalous white tucked back in the shade of alcoves and dikes, remnants of a freak spring storm that blew through just over a week ago (with the errant jaguar). Now, up here in the abiding north-side shade, hard against the massif, the slippery damned stuff is everywhere. Soon the trail disappears entirely beneath deep, then deeper, ice-crusted drifts. The going gets increasingly treacherous and I (wisely, Caroline will concur) give it up—even as Abbey was forced by snow to abandon his premier Baboquivari attempt.

So be it.

Having reached the end of the trail (for now), I make a little speech—to myself, I suppose—then use my trusty hiking staff (an antique bamboo ski pole) to scratch two words and a clandestine symbol into the snow. A message for a friend who (who knows?) might just pass this way.

With my Baboquivari pilgrimage behind me, I return to camp, the ever-sweet Caroline … and whatever awaits us down the trail.

14

Raid at Comb Wash, Redux

One fine day in early June, bearing west from Blanding, Utah ... the
gang paused at the summit of Comb Ridge for a look at the world
below. ... Comb Ridge is a great monocline, rising gradually on the
east side, dropping off at an angle close to ninety degrees on the west
side. The drop-off from the rim is about five hundred feet straight
down, with another three hundred feet or more of steeply sloping talus
below the cliff. Like many other canyons, mesas, and monoclines in
southeast Utah, Comb Ridge forms a serious barrier to east-west land
travel. Or it used to. God meant it to.

—Edward Abbey, "The Raid at Comb Wash,"
from *The Monkey Wrench Gang*

ONE FINE DAY IN early April, Branson and I descend into Owl
Creek Canyon, just west of the denticulate monolithic cliffs of Comb
Ridge and the great Comb Wash below. Owl is one of five sandstone
clefts drained by Comb Wash—the others being Arch, Mule, Road
and Fish Creek. All are rugged, remote and sublime.

Like Shakespeare's Richard II (and that other tricky Dick), *down,
down we go.* But unlike those other guys, Branson and I are not
descending a throne in defeat. We are descending *into* a throne in triumph. But that bit comes later.

The Owl Creek trailhead is set in the midst of a rolling sea of slickrock, like petrified ocean swells, and surrounded by some of the Four

Corner's most prominent landmarks. Near in the north, just east of Natural Bridges National Monument, protrude the twin-butte Bear's Ears. Northeastward rise the Abajo Mountains and Elk Ridge. Far in the southeast, the Sleeping Ute snores eternally. On the afternoon horizon, Black Mesa broods.

It's beyond beautiful in every direction and the hiking is easy— until you come, soon and suddenly, to the brink of the world and begin the rocky plunge to the canyon floor hundreds of feet below.

The descent to Owl Creek is merely interesting for experienced day hikers. But strap a motel on your back and all is changed—balance and footing become critical. Slowly and gingerly, therefore—scrambling over boulders, stooping under piñon and juniper limbs, creeping across exposed slickrock slopes—you pick your way down.

Soon you spot a small prehistoric ruin perched on the west wall. Like hundreds more hereabouts, this ancient structure was built and occupied with great labor and likely a bit of existential angst, some eight centuries ago. In the closing years of the 11th century, the builders, the Anasazi … vanished.

Ignore this minor ruin and continue on—down, down—to a larger and better preserved pre-Puebloan structure set back in a shallow alcove at the canyon's head.

This time you stop, drop your pack on the trail, hop off a low ledge, and do the detour. Your reward is a well preserved kiva—a circular "clubhouse" room (usually subterranean but not this one) with mystical connotations. The kiva's roof—a layer-cake of beams, lattice, juniper bark and adobe (proto "Santa Fe style")—was long ago pulled off by looters. But the walls—though fragile and liable to collapse the next time some dork tries to climb them—remain intact. Inspect the ends of the roof logs lying atop the kiva walls and you'll see the beaver-bite marks of stone axes.

Behind the kiva squat three smaller structures, like giant beehives, also of stone and adobe. These are storage bins for corn dried on the cob, the Anasazi manna. Capping the hatch to one of the bins is a thin, hand-shaped slab of sandstone. The sense of another time, another world, another worldview, is palpable. You can almost hear old Kokopelli, the hunch-backed backdoor man of local legend, tooting his flute.

The first time Branson brought Caroline and me here, years ago, it was winter and snow was falling in huge wobbly flakes, lending a quiet surrealism to the view down the red-and-white-striped abyss. Today is likewise stormy, if not so brisk. Virga—tufted curtains of moisture that never reach the ground—drape a gun-metal southern horizon. The desert smells like rain.

Tempting as it is to dally in this place of lurking spirits, it's afternoon already and the troubled heavens impart a sense of urgency. Having touched nothing and leaving only tracks in the ancient dust, we return to our packs and carry on.

Within the hour the gloom has lifted.

The sun stood high in the clouds; the air was still and warm.

From far below rises the sparkling voice of a canyon wren, each note a diamond. For those who know and love Abbey Country, the pellucid voice of *Catherpes mexicanus* is more than a joy, it is a benediction. What the loon gives the north country, the canyon wren brings to canyon country. And that *what* is magic.

We complete the descent without mishap and loaf on down-creek. Only a few miles along, just below the first big pour-off, we come to a campsite too good to pass. We have three days to enjoy a hike of only twenty miles or so—down Owl to its confluence with Fish Creek Canyon at Comb Wash, up Fish to the climb-out, then a short stroll back to the trailhead—so where's the hurry?

I dub this place Dragon Tree Amphitheater in honor of the convoluted cottonwood guarding its entrance. Like everything else in these canyons, the tree is ageless. Its trunk is a solid five feet through and forked. One big subtrunk undulates along the ground to frame the cloistered campsite. The other rises above our heads (the dragon's back), then dips sharply (its neck) and rises again (head) before drooping and tapering in a long pointy snout. From the dragon's head protrude a pair of horns.

We guess the amphitheater to be a hundred yards deep, half that wide and twice as high. Its vertical walls are sculpted from Cedar Mesa sandstone in alternating bands of rose and gray. In the back of the grotto glints a shallow pool. Its water is the color of China tea and supplied by a seep that slithers down a slickrock slot and trickles, tinkling like a hundred crystal bells, over two stone ledges to the pool thirty feet below. From sedimentary seams in the walls encircling the pool hang a profusion of spring columbines, just now going green and soon to flower in flaming red.

The afternoon sun flares bright as quicksilver on the mirrored pool. The drip-fall tinkles hypnotically. Just above the canyon rim one raven, insignificant against a vast azure sky, babbles at the universe. Higher, an anonymous raptor soars in easy arcs.

One thin scream came floating down, like a feather, from the silver-clouded sky ... solitaire, one hawk passing far above the red reef, above the waves of Triassic sandstone.

Driftwood, washed down by periodic flash-floods, is abundant in the main canyon, and my fuel collecting takes me there. Looking south, I spot a motley crew of monolithic sandstone hoodoos standing eternal guard—two sphinxes, one potbellied mummy and an owl as big as a five-story building.

Stooping for a stick of wood, I almost tromp a stamp-sized shard of pinched-coil pottery. I inspect the fragile fragment, wondering at the stories it knows, then return it to the earth. Happily burdened with firewood, I return campward.

As per usual, Branson announces his intent to sleep out tonight. Unswayed by this blatant display of *machismo*, I pitch my tent—I lugged the heavy bastard down here, I'll lug it back up, and I don't intend to see it go to waste. That done, I torch my little alcohol stove and boil water to rehydrate dinner (so-called). Branson busies himself cleaning out the hearth.

The previous campers left not a tatter of litter, bless them, but filled in their fire ring with rocks and sand. A wilderness no-no, this, since the next tenants, rather than cleaning out the sooty pit, will likely build a fresh one. And fill *it* in when *they* leave. In no time, hearths and ashes are everywhere and another pristine campsite is ruined.

Evening.

Now the stillness was complete. The watchers ... eating their suppers from tin plates, heard the croon of a mourning dove far down the wash. ... The great golden light of the setting sun streamed across the sky, glowing upon the clouds and the mountains. Almost all the country within their view was roadless, uninhabited, a wilderness. They meant to keep it that way.

At dusk we are treated to a private rock concert when a canyon wren invades the amphitheater and commences singing his (or her) pointy little head off, the fluted music enhanced to heavenly proportions by the eerie acoustics of this stony place.

Come full darkness the wren falls quiet, replaced by a duo of bass-voiced frogs—from the sound of it, a mating pair.

"Come-ere."

"No way!"

"Come-ere!"

"Okay!"

The friggin' frogs frolic late into the night, real party animals. The wind rises sporadically, blowing sand and big dollops of rain against my nylon abode. Too far off for thunder, heat lightning pulses. I toss restlessly through it all, while out there on his beloved dirt, the unflappable Branson (all six-foot-two of him) snores on.

❧

The dawn sky is clean and filled with promise, prompting us to hit the trail at the crack of midmorning. I use the term "trail" loosely, recalling a comment scribbled by a returned hiker in the trailhead register:

"More signs, please!"

In fact, *one* sign would be more—and one too many. This is a place for adventure, for getting lost and finding your own way out, for following footprints in the sand and cairns across slickrock. I thank the canyon gods that the Bureau of Land Management doesn't share the Forest Service's compulsion (or, perhaps, budget) for coddling a dilettante public and insulting the scenery with "More signs, please!"

As we walk, we play Name the Flora. We're a month too early for the best of it—precious few flowers are out just yet, the cottonwoods have barely begun to leaf and the browns of winter still dominate. Even so, we have the ubiquitous verdure of piñon pine and Utah juniper (known together by locals as "the P-J"), plus Mormon tea, buffalo berry, yucca like nests of spears, an occasional sanguine bouquet of Indian paintbrush, a few lavender vetch, some homely locoweed and several unknown varieties of little yellow flowers.

In places along the creek we wade through thickets of cattails and *Equisetum*. The latter—a reed best known as horsetail—erupts here (and there) dense as dog hair and higher than our heads, creating an atmosphere more evocative of a Southeast Asian jungle than the American Southwest.

We come to another pour-off. Below its ledge lies what Branson calls Deep Pool. Here the little creek plunges thirty feet to a pond I guess to be twenty yards across and so deep it's hard even to imagine a bottom. What mysteries lurk in those timeless smoky depths?

"I dove as deep as I could once," Branson confirms, "went halfway to hell but couldn't find bottom."

Here, as at Dragon Tree, the walls encircling the pool drip green with leafing columbines. Yard-long clumps of dry bunchgrass hang inverted from the rusty cliffs and bright new dandelions enliven the narrow beach. Also on that beach, a pair of slate-gray dippers perform their dips (like feathered lizards), then take wing and away, chirruping gaily.

After a while we work our way up along a ledge and down below the pool to an oasis of cottonwoods, naked now but on the verge of shading an idyllic campsite. Only thing missing from this picture, observes my friend (a career bachelor), is a long-haired nymph basking in the midday sun. Branson's in no hurry to leave ("Who knows when that nymph might show?"), but the day is young and the trail is long ahead.

With a couple more miles under our boots, we round a bend and meet, towering to port astern, the Cameo Lady: hair pulled back in a modest bun, eyes closed, face downcast, coy and demur. She is the most realistic natural stone sculpture I've ever seen, shaped and honed by eons of mindless meteorology. She is also our signal to camel-up: we're nearing the lower canyon and for the next few miles, warns Branson, water is reliably unreliable.

When we come to a pool a foot deep and clear, we drop our packs, I fish out my old cheap filter pump from my old cheap pack and we squat and pump and drink until our teeth float, then pump some more to top off the bottles. Finished, standing, I slip and fall in.

As I'm changing into dry socks, Branson tells a story. "It was right here," he begins, "where I made my most amazing wildlife observation ever. I was just sitting and looking around, when here comes a tiger swallowtail—the lemon-yellow kind with delicate black pin-striping. As the butterfly went flitting by, I noticed that right behind it, right on its tail, was a *bat*, the pair of them flying in perfect formation."

"A bat chasing a butterfly, in broad daylight yet; amazing."

"There's more. A minute later, here they came back. And this time, the butterfly is tailgating the bat!"

Believe it or not. (Knowing Branson, I do.)

In due course we round another bend in the canyon walls and there it is—the Owl Creek denouement—a massive rock rainbow called Nevill's Arch. Bent across the top of a hanging side-canyon, it's big enough to fly a 727 through (maybe).

And more. Arrayed along the cliff to the south of the arch is a giant's gallery of hoodoos: a squatting frog, a Mexican hat, a bearded sheik with turban-wrapped head, and a phallus (only half erect but sixty feet tall at that).

We stare a good long while, then plod reluctantly on.

Reluctant because just below Nevill's Arch the canyon walls retreat and the valley floor flattens and the slickrock disappears beneath deep, dusty sand. No water nowhere. We are approaching the confluence—the least enjoyable leg of the hike. Yet it's also the "triumphant" bit alluded to earlier and, for me, the motivation for this visit.

The confluence is a dry, shadeless sagebrush flat bristling with thistle, snakeweed, rabbitbrush, cheatgrass, locoweed, tumbleweed and other noxious invaders symptomatic of overgrazing. Prickly pear abounds. The stream banks are trampled, eroded, denuded of riparian greenery, and the channel runs wide and talc-dry. Fine red dust coats our skin and grits in our eyes.

Yet—the point being—in spite of all these symptoms and more of a tragic history of "wise use" abuse by ranchers and their lackeys at BLM, it's a hell of a lot better here now than it was just a couple of years ago—because the cows and their keepers have been given the boot.

Likewise the other canyons of Comb Wash. And in attaining this ecological reprieve, I played a role. A tiny role relative to others, to be sure, but a role nonetheless. These cowless, healing canyons offer palpable proof that concerned, tenacious individuals—the proverbial little guys and girls—*can* make a difference.

In March 1988, just after the winter grazing season, Joseph Feller, a professor at Arizona State University in Tempe, took a hike in Arch Canyon. What Feller saw there, he'll tell you, was "appalling ... cow pies everywhere. The vegetation had all been grazed down to

root-stubble. The stream banks and cryptobiotic crust were trampled and destroyed. It looked like a war zone." Feller headed home
determined to *do* something.

What he did was appeal BLM's Comb Wash grazing practices to
BLM's mother agency, the U.S. Department of the Interior. As a result,
DoI administrative law judge John R. Rampton, Jr., directed the area
BLM boss to explain and reconsider his Comb Wash grazing strategy.
Digging in the heels of his cowboy boots, the BLM manager ignored
the court's mandate and issued another grazing permit, without
modifications, to the Ute Mountain Utes. (Indians as cowboys: the
ironic New West.)

No quitter, this tenacious feller Joe recruited the National Wildlife
Federation and the Southern Utah Wilderness Alliance (together, the
"appellants") to join in filing a second, much broader appeal. Rallying
'round the BLM were the usual suspects: the American Farm Bureau
Federation, the Public Lands Council (a "wise use" euphemism), the
National Cattlemen's Association, the American Sheep Industry Association (of course!), the Ute Mountain Ute Indian Tribe et al. (the
"respondents").

I knew roughly what was going down and had written a few letters
on behalf of Comb Wash. Somehow and eventually, I was invited to
testify regarding the condition of my favorite Cedar Mesa retreat—a
secluded spring at the head of a Comb Wash side canyon—before
and after a recent winter of abusive grazing.

The upshot of it all was a rare sweet victory in the ongoing battle
for public control of public lands. Witness a few excerpts from Judge
Rampton's findings, decisions and relief orders:

"BLM failed to comply with NEPA [National Environmental
Policy Act]. ...

"BLM has not made a reasoned and informed decision that the
benefits of grazing the canyons outweigh the costs. ...

"BLM has violated the grazing regulations by issuing grazing
authorizations without consulting with affected interests. ...

"BLM is hereby prohibited from allowing any grazing in the canyons until an adequate EIS [Environmental Impact Statement] is prepared and considered [and] until BLM makes a reasoned and informed decision that grazing the canyons is in the public interest. ..."

Etcetera and hallelujah!

If Cactus Ed were here today, I know absolutely that he'd be shouting praises from every canyon rim for Fightin' Joe Feller and his allies at the National Wildlife Federation. And rightly so, for these brave few, with help from several unnamed but significant others, have returned this desert Eden to the American public.

One brave act is worth a thousand brave words.

So said Ed, frequently, by way of belittling his own massive contributions. And also because he believed it. What I learned from my Comb Wash experience is that brave words *are* brave acts.

∾

As we round the bend and head up the dry bed of Fish Creek, Branson and I tally the evidence of self-resurrection since the cowboys were cowed. (I love a thick pink steak as much as the next cholesterol junkie. But the western public lands produce an insignificant 2 percent of the red meat consumed in the U.S. annually, at an unconscionable cost to the environment, local economies, recreation and peace in the valley.)

What few cow-plops remain are so desiccated they no longer smell, squish underfoot or attract the flies that for decades made this place a hiker's hell. (Pie fly: the official bird of the "wise use" movement.) Native grasses are fighting their way back, as are wildflowers and other forbs.

With more food available, wildlife is also returning. As we walk we count the prints of deer, coyotes, rabbits, lizards, ring-tailed cats and more. In places, even the cryptobiotic crust—a delicate, lichenlike organic growth on the soil's surface that holds moisture, slows erosion and aids plant growth—is rejuvenating. Give it another hundred years. Please.

Lunch break. While we're chowing, a breeze puffs up and stiffens and the sky grays over—grayest in the north of course, the way we're headed.

Sated, we continue up Fish Creek. Long before our bottles run dry we strike water, an isolated pool from which two gorgeous green-heads rise and flap away, quacking their umbrage. More pools, then a living creek, and soon we come to the first in an emerald chain of beaver ponds, a welcome anomaly in this semi-desert. In the shallow depths of these natural reservoirs lurk the fish for which this place was named, minnowy little suckers and shiners for the most part.

The breeze becomes a wind. The sky grows darker. We bull ahead, but soon are forced to seek refuge from a twenty-knot blow and raindrops that sting like hail. Our port in this sudden storm is a huge boulder with one side deeply undercut by erosion. Atop this giant pebble—fifteen feet above the canyon floor—rests the bleached corpse of a mature cottonwood ... flash flood? The boulder alcove keeps the rain out, if not the blowing sand. True grit.

This turn of events is, we agree (searching for a silver lining), modestly exciting. But before long the worst of the storm blows on, and so do we.

In late afternoon we encounter the first humanoids we've seen in three days, a boisterous crew of two middle-aged men and a dozen teen-age boys—headed (we give silent thanks) in the opposite direction.

As we pass and mumble mutual hellos, I notice the boys looking at Branson kind of funnylike and snickering. One precocious brat even grins and winks. Mystified, I turn to my buddy and for the first time notice his "lipstick"—a bright red stain encircling his mouth ... from the quart of cherry Kool Aid he swigged with lunch, no doubt.

"Hey," I announce to the world, stepping back, "I'm not with *him*."

The boys laugh. I laugh. Branson appears puzzled. We all move along. When we're out of earshot, I reveal the joke to my baffled pal, suggesting that before we return to civilization he might want to wash his face. "Maybe," says he, trying to gain the upper hand. But too late: he is for the duration of this trip Lipstick Man.

It's evening when we make camp on a sandy bench near a slender slickrock pool. Should it come another rain, the site offers a small alcove with a stone hearth-ring sheltered beneath.

But it doesn't.

Twilight creeps yellow up the eastern wall. A canyon wren sings on cue. We kindle a fire of juniper and bathe in the stream of its tangy smoke. Life is good.

The evening gave way to night, a dense violet solution of starlight and darkness mixed with energy, each rock and shrub and tree and scarp outlined by an aura of silent radiation.

And a halcyon night she is, the stars bright as hope, dense and delicious as red-eye gravy. Sleep comes fast and stays long.

∿

A clear cool dawn. We squander a luxurious two hours on breakfast, packing and general geeking around, loathe to leave.

An hour up-canyon, we pause to ponder a panel of pictographs decorating an alcove to the east—big white paintings on a red sandstone palette: From left to right I discern a serpent, an inverted L, a row of inverted pyramids, a circle of five pyramids all pointed inward (like the petals of some magical flower), a P and another pyramid flower.

Go figure.

The canyon forks. We keep left. Soon we come to yet another inviting campsite, this one perched above a small, cattail-fringed drip pool. Here the trail jumps a head-high ledge, demanding the removal of our packs; Branson climbs up, I pass up the packs and scramble after.

Now the way levels out, leading to one last lovely pool, this one florid with early blooming cave primrose (good old *Primula specuicola*). Each delicate lavender flower, I note, consists of five triangular petals, the points facing in. (The *déjà* view.) A hummingbird, my first sighting of the year, goes ringing past, an iridescent blur.

From the primrose pool it's all uphill—in places, almost vertically so—hundreds of feet worth. Twice more we're forced to doff our packs and hand them up, and once a short rope-haul is required. This "trail" up and out of Fish Creek Canyon is not merely steep, it's hard to follow and not infrequently dangerous.

"More signs, please!" we shout, laughing at the knee-knocking irony.

At the rim (at last), breathless from more than just the prolonged exertion, I announce to Lipstick Man that I would never *de*scend this route wearing a backpack (down is always trickier than up), though others likely do it all the time. Branson—who could have been a high-wire artist—says nothing, only grins his bright red grin. He's done it many's the time before (just last week, in fact), and will do it again without pause.

To each his own poison. There are worse ways to go, and there are certainly worse places in which to go. Almost anyplace, in fact.

From the rim of Fish Creek Canyon back to the trailhead is a mesa-top stroll through an enchanted garden of old-growth P-J. We walk in silence (if not in grace)—exhausted, content, humbly triumphant.

15

A Place Where Spirits Dwell

IT'S NIGHT ALREADY down in the sandstone canyons of south-eastern Utah, though twilight still lingers up here on the rim, where my little camp is set near a vertical stone gash plunging a thousand feet into ... what? I hope never to find out. I've come here to this ancient stone heart of the Southwest alone, pack on back, as I do every once in a while, seeking recreation, relaxation, solitude. Nothing more is expected, nothing less is likely.

As I sit gazing into a sparking campfire, it occurs to me that to some clouded eyes, the rocky, semidesert landscape that comprises much of the Colorado Plateau must seem desolate, foreboding, more dead than alive. Not true. It's just that life hereabouts doesn't flaunt itself.

Visible to anyone who cares to look are a wealth of diurnal creatures: the turquoise sky virtually swarms with bird life: darting cliff swallows, bell-voiced canyon wrens, swifts graceful in aerobatic flight, hawks, falcons, eagles, vultures, blue-black iridescent ravens ... while here on the ground, the shade of piñon, juniper and sage hides deer, rabbits, ground squirrels, lizards, snakes, the stodgy desert tortoise and myriad others.

And come the darkness, you need only listen to discover life. Even now, as I sit here fireside and muse, a great-horned owl's persistent query animates the night. The owl is answered by a melancholy nightjar—*Poor Will, Poor Will.* Some small, unseen mammal scurries amongst the sagebrush beyond the campfire's little cave of light.

And always, above, around and through it all, rings a cacophony of crickets.

I let the fire burn to coals, roll out my nylon sleep-sack on the warm soft sand and prepare for the "little death." No tent, and no need for one; out here, on a sublime spring night such as this, the luminous heavens are shelter enough. I drift to sleep steeped in the incense fragrance of smoldering piñon.

∾

Waking to a morning made for hiking, I strike off south along an undulating canyon rim of erosion-sculpted sandstone, a terrain looking for all the world like an ocean of petrified waves. My destination, a couple of miles distant, lies hidden beneath an overhung aerie surveying a broad canyon floor a quarter-mile below. To find the place, you have to know it's there. A long time ago, Branson brought me here. Keeping the faith, I've shared it with few others— a secret too widely known loses its magic.

At the promontory, I lower myself through a split in the rim rock, then skid and slide down a steep talus slope to a narrow ledge a hundred feet below. Hugging the ledge across a vertical cliff face, trying not to look down, I emerge all weak and shaky at the mouth of a shallow alcove … a place where spirits dwell.

Three hundred years before Columbus sailed, an extended family, or clan, of stone age natives lived in this west-facing rock shelter. The Navajo who occupy this arid land today call them *Anasazi* (ancient ones), though anthropologists and others swayed by the current rage for political correctness are attempting to substitute the demystifying and sterile term "pre-Puebloans."

In addition to building sturdy pueblos of adobe and hand-shaped sandstone blocks, the Anasazi hunted, gathered wild foods, farmed and fired fine painted pottery, black on white. Offering mute evidence of their skill and prolificity as potters, palm-sized shards of mugs, jugs, bowls and ladles lie strewn about the alcove floor. I pick up a few pieces, admiring their geometric designs—yet clean and sharp, refuting seven centuries of wind, rain and sun. One at a time, I return the shards to their rightful place—not in some natty "museum" pile atop a rock, as children and Tourons are wont to do, but scattered like memories in the dust.

Amazingly, a few desiccated corncobs also survive, dehydrated and shrunken by the arid climate. These are the produce of a crop grown and harvested even as Kublai Khan and his Mongol masses ran amok through Asia … even as a dreary Europe suffered through the unthinkable horrors of its Middle Ages.

What might have prompted these enigmatic people to nest on such risky aeries as this and hundreds of similar others all across the Four Corners region of the American Southwest? The daily chores of hauling in food, water and firewood along that hellish entrance ledge would have been onerous, even life-threatening. And with only a few yards of sloping rock between your home and the abyss of eternity, you could never allow your children out of sight, or hand, for even a moment. (Not, at least, if you liked them.)

Why *did* the Anasazi become cliff dwellers?

A strong clue in this instance (as in so many similar others) is a tumble-down defensive wall erected across the narrowest span of the approach ledge. A portal in its center is just large enough to allow one person at a time to squeeze slowly through. A lone sentry stationed out there, armed with stone club, spear or atlatl, could beat back a small army of invaders as they attempted, one doomed fool at a time, to wriggle through.

Obviously, like the overwhelming majority of Anasazi cliff dwellings elsewhere—especially the smaller, more isolated sites— this place was selected for its all-around security; a fortress hidden against unknown ancient enemies … transient raiders up from Old

Mexico? ... internecine rivals from neighboring Anasazi clans? ... roving bands of outlaw outcasts? I go with the latter.

Certainly, by the time this stone retreat was built, the Anasazi had enjoyed so much growth and progress that they'd all but grown themselves out of business. Trees had been over-cut for timber and fuel, wildlife had been over-hunted, the sparse sandy soil over-farmed, the human population—thought to have been even larger then than now—had swelled far beyond the carrying capacity of the local ecology. And then, beginning in 1145 and lasting through 1190, came the *coup de grâce,* the Great Drought.

It was during those bad years—during the time this little enclave was built and occupied—that the Anasazi cultural, trade and architectural center at Chaco Canyon, in nearby New Mexico, collapsed (socially if not physically) and was abandoned ... and that unknown raiders, most likely crazed Anasazi, on occasion murdered, butchered, cooked and ate entire Anasazi families. Such slaughter sites have been scientifically documented throughout the Four Corners.

Why? My money is on social stress arising from nutritional stress arising from overpopulation, environmental depletion and drought. "Grow or die" has become the rallying cry for everyone from small-town chambers of commerce to national leaders. But for the Anasazi (as it has been and will be for countless others), it was *grow until you die.*

I stoop into one of the four almost identical, low-roofed rooms— rectangular, just large enough to accommodate a couple of adults and maybe a child or two. I find that I can sit comfortably, but standing is impossible; the ceiling—which consists of nothing more than the sloping alcove roof—is quite low. A single small door/window looks west across the canyon. Fire-blackened inner walls and ceiling confirm that this tiny chamber was used as a living space. A row of wooden pegs spaced at about six-inch intervals jut from the crumbling mud-plaster high along the inner walls—pegs from which once hung buckskin bags and woven-fiber baskets containing valued personal belongings, talismans, ceremonial magic. Or perhaps the pegs supported a narrow shelf.

Feeling gritty and claustrophobic inside the tiny cubicle, I crawl back out into the dazzling southwestern sunshine and continue my respectful poking around.

Tucked back into the narrow, pinched-off rear of the alcove at either end of the row of connected cells are a matched pair of rounded, guano-glazed granaries. One has an inch-thick, hand-shaped sandstone slab—a door—leaned against its small opening. In the dust of the granary floor lie scattered a few mummified corncobs and the hard black pellets of wood rats.

I move away from the ruins, toward the cliff's edge, and seat myself at the center of a sunken bowl of earth circled by a tumbled wall of sandstone blocks. Beneath me (I know from having seen many such places, before and after excavation) lies a collapsed kiva, an underground ceremonial chamber. In this little pueblo's heyday, down in this dark, smoky cellar, the men of the clan would have gathered to talk, sing, smoke and perform clandestine ceremonies. This we know for certain, for even today the Pueblo peoples of New Mexico and Arizona—direct descendants of the "pre-Puebloans"—practice similar rites in similar kivas.

Seduced by the haunting atmosphere of this place, I consider spending the night—it would be, well, an *experience*—but quickly think better of it. There is no firewood, I have no real food and not enough water. Besides, respect demands leaving these musty old ruins to the juniper-scented ghosts of the people who, for reasons perhaps less recondite than those that brought them here, one day just walked away from it all, deserting a native homeland considered by them as *Sipapu*—the womb of humanity.

Bottom line: the Anasazi are gone. And now I too must leave.

I brush out my tracks in the dust of the alcove floor, hug back along the cliff-hanging trail, ease over the crumbled defensive wall, scramble back up the talus slope, squeeze myself up through the cleft to the canyon rim and take the scenic route home. (Out here on this enchanted rolling seascape of rose and buff sandstone, azure sky and blue-green piñon-juniper, *every* route is the scenic route.)

∞

I sag into camp at dusk, drop my pack and slump down to the living heart of this dusty place—a drip-spring cloistered in a shaded grotto at the head of a small side canyon. Uncapping my two parched canteens, I place them on the sand beneath a slow line of diamond droplets emerging from a seam in the sandstone wall. There is no sweeter music, Abbey said, than the *tink-tink, tink* of desert water dripping into a tin cup. And there is no sweeter taste, I would add, than cool spring water and a splash of Irish whiskey sipped within the perfumed smoke of a P-J campfire in the American Southwest on a mild spring night.

As the day dims and the drip-spring drips, drips, in no hurry whatsoever to satisfy my impatient thirst, I stand staring in wonder at this place. Here, as in uncounted similar oases flung by geologic happenstance far and wide across the Colorado Plateau, grow anomalous riparian plant communities utterly dependent for their survival on scant moisture leaking improbably from "solid" rock. Like the biblical burning bush, desert drip springs are miracles in the wilderness—miracles you can drink.

Here, as in so many canyon-country elsewheres, carpeting the damp grotto wall along and below the drip line are lush mosses. And thriving in and around the pellucid spring pool are cattails, ferns, reeds, Indian paintbrush, and one saucy, red-lipped monkey-flower.

At my feet, the damp sand rimming the pool is a journal of wildlife activity. From the tracks I read that a rabbit, various tiny rodents, a fox and an adult mule deer have been here recently. The usual lot of thirsty desert mammals.

But wait ... that's not all.

In the periphery of my vision I notice an odd depression in the damp sand and step over to investigate. My pocket flashlight cuts through the twilight to reveal a track as big as a big man's hand—much larger than any coyote, though not so big as a bear—and rounded, with no claw marks visible. The bi-lobed front edge and tri-lobed rear of the plantar pad are clearly distinguished and irrefutably indicative ... cougar. The single print is sharp-edged and fresh. I look around but can find no others; apparently, the cat ventured just this one step off the slickrock toward the spring, then withdrew.

My skin prickles with the knowledge that one of the largest and most perfect predators in North America has been here, *right here,* and not all that long ago—a beast of the magical clan popularly and rightly referred to as "charismatic megafauna."

I drop to my knees and read the track from every angle, then stand again and point the little flashlight all around. But the batteries are weak and the tired yellow beam doesn't reach far. In another minute or so, both twilight and flashlight will fade completely, and I'll be left here in the dark. Alone ... or perhaps not. A chill sprints along my spine.

Be cool, man. Like the old saw says, there's nothing to fear but ... what? Why is it we tend to fear the unseen more than the visible, the unknown more than the known, the uncertain more than the absolute?

Statistically, you are several *hundred* times less likely to be attacked by a mountain lion than to be struck by lightning. May be. But *you* aren't here, *I* am, there isn't a storm cloud in sight and the biggest cougar track I've ever seen is fresh at my feet and my heart is pounding in my throat.

I snatch up the two sloshing, half-filled canteens in one hand—the quart they hold between them will have to suffice until morning—clutch the increasingly impotent flashlight in the other hand and scurry back to camp and the comforts of home and hearth.

After replacing the spent flashlight batteries with spares from my pack, I distract myself with evening camp chores: spread ground-cloth, sleeping pad and bag on the sand—a bit nearer the fire than last night—kindle a blaze, boil water for tea, scorch and devour a big bloody elk steak brought from home—frozen yesterday, way beyond thawed now. We sure don't need no stinkin' lion bait lying around tonight.

Much later, I toss a final club of piñon onto the big pile of coals, strip and slide into the cocoonish security of my sleeping bag. Just me, ten thousand desert stars above and two little brown bats—Mexican free-tails, I presume—turning and diving after the confused multitude of moths circling at the fading edges of firelight. (I think fondly of Christine, bat biologist. I'll have to bring her here someday.)

Brooding over that big round track down by the spring, sleep is a long time coming.

But sleep I do—until about midnight, when a family of coyotes wakes me, yammering maniacally, sounding close but probably not. The fire is as dead as old love, the world as black as eternity. I manage to keep my eyes open just long enough to witness one blue-green shooting star make an ambitious rush for the western horizon, only to burn itself out in the trying.

∾

When the dream comes, it's almost palpable—no clear images, only blackness and eerie, suspiring, susurrus sounds ... like the guarded footfalls of a prowler ... a rapid, rhythmic respiration.

Feeling vaguely threatened by the ethereal sounds, I come half-awake and rise on my elbows. Though I'm warm in my bag, I notice that my arms are pimpled with goose flesh. I peer into the darkness but see nothing. I listen, but no sound comes. All is quiet in the anthracite desert night. The stars have dimmed and even the owls and crickets have hushed. I consider switching on the flashlight for a look around but don't, for fear I'll think myself a coward come morning. Finally, feeling a little foolish, I lie back and wait for sleep to return.

∾

In the amber glow of dawn I wake all bleary-eyed and groggy to discover that my eerie dream was in fact no dream at all. There in the powdery sand, just a body's length out from my sleeping place, imprinted over one of my own boot marks, is a big round track.

I unzip my bag, stand and look around. The prints are everywhere. Over there, the lion approached from the sage. And those odd marks show where he, or she, sat back on lean haunches, long tail sweeping a fan-shaped arc in the sand. From that reflective repose I imagine the prowler staring at me with big nocturnal eyes, listening, inhaling my sweat scent, panting softly, pondering the redolent sleeper in inscrutable feline fashion.

As best I can read the spoor, it appears the lion then moved to the far side of the fire pit and haunch-sat again. And over there, its curiosity apparently satisfied—or maybe I startled it with my sudden awakening—the cat padded back into the sage. Perhaps it *remains* nearby, biding its time, biding mine.

Following a sudden and reckless urge, I pull on shorts, lace boots over sockless feet and follow the departing trail. But the prints soon strike slickrock and that's that.

Warmed by strong camp coffee and relaxed under a brilliant morning sun, I sit and reflect. Had the cat been looking to make a meal of me, it likely could have. Pumas are predation perfected, capable of bringing down not just deer, but creatures as large as elk and cattle and horses … and on very rare occasion, people. Stalking close, then pouncing after a short rush, the cougar kills by sinking long canines into the skull or neck of the startled victim, then holding, holding. An unarmed naked sleeper would barely know what hit him or her.

Obviously, predation was not the prowler's intent. Or, drawing near, the keen-nosed animal was offended by my multi-day trail smell. Probably both. Most likely, I spooked it off the spring last night and it's been lurking nearby since, curious as a cat. Was I in any real danger? I'll never know for certain. And just as well.

I am not a spiritual person in any orthodox, or for that matter unorthodox sense. Magical thinking of any stripe sends me searching for the nearest exit to reality. What I can see, hear, smell, taste and touch is plenty good enough for me. Yet, out here in the ancient dust, here among Anasazi ghosts and nocturnal dream creatures, here in the pulsing heart of the West—here in this place where spirits dwell—I feel that my life has been touched by magic.

ᖰ

POSTSCRIPT: I recently returned to the "lion camp" with a special guest. Her name is Christine, and from the day she was born, she's been like a daughter to me.

Just before leaving her San Francisco home to come out West (*sic*) for our long-planned reunion/camping adventure, Chris read the account recorded above. And now, sitting beside me near a crackling fire in the selfsame spot where that story unfolded, she turns to me and asks, "Dad, did you *really* see a mountain lion here?"

"No," I respond truthfully, and perhaps a little brusquely, disappointed that she would doubt me, "I didn't *see* it."

"But you saw its tracks; it was here?"

"Yes, I saw lion tracks; it was here."

Next morning, while I rehabilitate the fire for coffee, Chris walks down to the spring for water. When she returns, a rosy blush colors her cheeks.

"Dad," says she, a glint in her big brown eyes, "I have something to show you; and would you please bring your camera?"

Chris goes for her own camera, then, without question, I follow her back to the sandstone cul-de-sac, past the spring to a shallow pool of water not far below. There, imprinted clear as truth in the damp sand beside the water, are two huge, round, perfect … lion tracks.

"These weren't here last evening," says my delighted kinder.

"No, they weren't."

"Let's both take pictures," Chris suggests, "just in case anyone might ever doubt us."

16

Yellowstone Death Watch

"I'LL GUARANTEE YA," says my new friend Jason Wilson, "the first time you see it, you'll get a rush that'll surpass anything in your entire pharmaceutical history."

Of my pharmaceutical history, this charismatic carpenter and farmer from Virginia could hardly know much, considering we've only just met. But of the "rush" in question, he speaks with unimpeachable authority: Jason and his lively wife Debbie Lineweaver, a teacher and management consultant, have been making annual pilgrimages to Yellowstone National Park for the past quarter of a century, addicted to the gruesome sort of natural high they're tripping over one another to recount for me now.

"It was a grizzly sow with cubs," says Debbie.

"And a month-old elk calf," says Jason.

"It was crazy," says Debbie, "like the Keystone Cops."

"For a while there," says Jason, "it looked like the calf was in the clear, then ..."

"Now hold on," I protest. "Let's hear it all of a piece."

"OK," says Jason, who gets the nod from Debbie and begins. "We were glassing in the Antelope Creek area when we spotted a grizzly sow with a pair of big yearling cubs. Right away the sow jumped an elk calf from hiding. The calf was old enough to sprint like a greyhound, and round and round they went."

"Then here comes the mother elk," says Debbie, unable to hold her peace, "charging in and barking and harassing the sow until she left off chasing the calf and just sort of stood there, dazed-looking. At that point, the calf was free and clear."

"But it apparently mistook the grizzly sow for its own mom," says Jason, "because it ran in a big circle and right back around, smack into the bear."

"That old sow just reached out, casual like, and smacked the calf a keeper, and that was that," says Jason. "The cubs ran over to join their ma and with the three of them going at it, that calf made the metabolic journey within minutes. What a *rush* to witness! Deb and I were so high on adrenaline, we were literally shaking in our boots. We've been back every spring since, looking to see more of the same."

Looking to see some of the same for ourselves, Caroline and I arrived here late yesterday. As soon as we'd set up camp, we climbed back in the truck and motored east along the Lamar Valley road, through Lamar Canyon, close above the thundering Lamar River and out into the fifteen-mile expanse of valley. Before dark, we'd made the acquaintance of Jason and Deb, two wolves and a grizzly bear.

In preparation for this trip, I'd called Rick McIntyre—writer, photographer, editor of the anthology *War Against Wolves* and a Park Service naturalist with two decades of close-up experience with potentially fierce creatures (wolves, bears, park bureaucrats, tourists) at Denali, Glacier and Yellowstone. I told Rick we were headed his way in hopes of witnessing the annual ritual of "big bad predators slaughtering innocent baby elk." We were prepared to backpack in as deep and long as necessary.

"Forget that," said Rick. "Leave your packs at home and bring your lawn chairs. Lamar Valley is the place; cruise the road watching for knots of parked vehicles and people with binoculars, spotting scopes and telephoto lenses. Look where everyone else is looking."

☙

Yellowstone's Lamar Valley is home to—who knows?—a couple thousand elk. In turn, the Lamar herd is part of the sprawling Northern Range herd, which comprises some eighteen thousand elk spread across 350 square miles—the largest distinct wad of wapiti in the world.

Each spring, from mid-May through mid-June (everywhere elk live, not just in Yellowstone), wapiti cows give birth to calves that hit the ground at a frail and wobbly average thirty-five pounds. For the first three weeks (or so), the newborns are unable to evade predators by running, so have evolved what biologists call the "hider" strategy.

Like so: As soon as a cow "drops," she devours the afterbirth to prevent its odor from attracting predators. Meanwhile and nearby, the near-scentless newborn assumes an instinctive hiding posture, curled on the ground and motionless except when nursing. When not actively tending her calf, the mother stands guard just within range of vocal communication (catlike mews and birdlike chirps), so that her own musky odor and hulking quarter-ton outline won't cue predators to the exact spot where her helpless calf is cowering.

Should a threat appear nearby, instinct prevents the infant from even blinking (literally). If the hunter gets dangerously close, the cow (if she has solid family values, which a few do not) comes rushing to the rescue in the way Deb and Jason described—neck extended like a camel, barking like a dog, trying to distract the killer without getting herself killed in the doing. If the infant's nerve holds and its mother is better at her job than the predator is at his, the calf will go undetected.

Every now and again, though, a cougar (not often observed, but always on the job), a bear, a coyote—or, as of 1995, a wolf—will discover a hider and dispatch it with a swipe of clawed paw or a viselike bite to the neck, extracting life for itself and its own posterity from the death of an elk calf. Not cuddly, anthropomorphic Disney nature, this, but nature red in tooth and claw. *Real* nature. To those who understand, it is beautiful beyond description.

ॐ

Across the decades, Yellowstone's bears have learned not only when and where to hunt wapiti, but how. The most common caper is the "slow search," wherein the hunter walks a grid through such likely calving grounds as aspen groves and sage flats. Park coyotes, as adaptable as they are wily and abundant, have learned to ape the bears' tactics, while the recently translocated wolves, wild to the heart, need no schooling.

By mid- to late June, most healthy elk calves are big enough to run with their mothers, and cow-calf pairs come together in mutually protective herds. Now, hungry predators are forced to adopt a more aggressive hunting tactic—charging into these "nursery" herds in a calamitous effort to separate calves from adults, hoping to single out a straggler. Quite the show for those watchers lucky or determined enough to see it.

By Independence Day, the Yellowstone Touron season ("Can't stay long; gotta tour on!") is at full tilt and the surviving calves—the healthiest, smartest and best-parented (thus, best-gened) of the annual lot—are reasonably safe from predation. Gradually, the bears return to digging roots, nipping wildflowers and knocking apart rotten logs in search of insects, while the coyotes, by and large, revert to dogging rodents and scavenging.

But now, with the return of the wolves, the spectator sport of predator-watching extends year-round. In winter—when the weakest ungulates are starving and deep snow slows their escape and even adult moose and bison can be vulnerable to snowshoe-pawed canids—sightings of wolves giving chase and making kills are frequent and poignant.

Life feeds on life: It's hard, but it works. And it's absolutely essential. Without predation, life on earth would spiral rapidly into oblivion. Where big predators exist in viable numbers atop a sturdy food pyramid, wild nature remains most nearly in balance.

Consider: After wolves were exterminated from Yellowstone in the late 1920s, elk and bison multiplied essentially unrestrained, to the point that some riparian areas today are seriously overgrazed. Most every winter, starving ungulates spill out of the park and onto private ranchlands, prompting fear and loathing among agrarian locals. Some relief came with the post-conflagration killer winter of 1988–89, which decreased park elk numbers by a third. But even this massive die-off failed to restore a natural and healthy ecological balance, and herds have been on the rise again since.

Too many prey; too few predators.

(Re)enter the wolves. The official restoration goal is ten breeding pairs (each heading a pack), for a total of roughly one hundred wolves operating throughout the Yellowstone ecosystem. These hungry hunters will have a bountiful large-mammal prey base—elk, deer, bison, moose, bighorns, pronghorns and mountain goats—of about a hundred-thousand animals. The wolves are expected to take 1.2 percent of this number per annum (yes, just one kill per wolf per month on average), mostly the old, infant and infirm, culling the weak and expendable, improving the quality of the herd while diminishing its quantity only marginally.

It's a kids-in-a-candy-store scenario for the big dogs: they're such obviously *happy campers* here, it's hard to imagine that many would choose to leave the park to "depredate" on boring old livestock that rarely even give the primal satisfaction of running when chased. And thus far, few have.

∾

A benevolent June morning. Caroline and I are up and on the go at sunrise, arriving in the valley in plenty of time to learn that we've just missed four griz strolling along the skyline. We're bummed, but only until two more bears appear on an exposed snow bank high on a ridge across the river. Incredibly, the grizzlies are attended by a huge gray wolf. They're a long way off, but clearly visible through my East German military surplus binoculars, and through a spotting scope they're breathtaking.

Now appears Ranger Rick, a regular at these roadside watches. Rick needs only a glance through my scope to determine that this is the alpha female of the Crystal Creek pack. The bears, obviously, are a mated pair engaged in courtship frolic.

At first, we think the wolf must be trying to hijack a kill from the bears—rushing at the sow and nipping her plump thighs, then darting away, prompting the June bride to take repeated leave of her lover to give chase. But there is no kill in sight.

Incredibly, we soon realize, without doubt, that the wolf is *playing* with the grizzlies. Even more incredible, the sow is playing back. Once, in mid-chase, the fleeing hundred-pound dog skids to a stop, whirls and counter-charges the four-hundred-pound bear ... who turns rump and runs.

As if staging a grand finale to their morning performance, the ursine lovers sit face-to-face, embrace in a bear hug and go tumbling down the snow bank, their log-thick limbs clumsily entangled and their pet wolf dancing along after. We are deeply saddened when this unlikely trio romps over the ridge and out of sight.

While all of this is happening, watchers a mile east are watching two wolves kill an elk calf out in the sage and drag it back into the woods—even as, farther south yet, a sibling pair of subadult grizzlies (the behavioral equivalent to human teen-agers) spend the morning combing an aspen grove across the river from the Lamar picnic area in search of wapiti veal, find some, and squabble over it to the mixed horror and delight of a dozen watchers before carrying it off to dine in privacy.

Even so, Caroline and I have had our share of excitement, and are content to spend the remainder of the morning just watching the watchers.

Like the strikingly gravity-challenged man who pulls up in a garish diesel van with a spotting scope mounted on the dash above the steering wheel, then spends an eternity maneuvering the noisy, noxious vehicle—backing up and pulling forward at various angles—so that he won't have to leave his seat to watch. He is literally aiming his scope with his van while the rest of us gag on his fumes. Just as one gray-bearded ex-Marine watcher is plotting mischief, Mr. Van Potato motors off, leaving in his wake an acrid cloud of diesel smoke.

And the young yuppie couple who come zipping up in a racy red convertible of European pedigree, top down. Both are dressed like L.L. Bean models and within seconds are on the watch, and on display. The tan young man peers through a spotting scope he slaps quickly into place on a window mount, while his leggy partner poses prettily atop the back of her bucket seat, peering through what look like opera glasses. But their attention span is as brief as the woman's shorts (I'm *not* complaining), and they soon buzz off to entertain the next wad of watchers up the way.

By contrast, the serious Yellowstone "observer community" is a community in fact, though hailing from wide and far. (From where I now sit, I can see plates from Montana, Virginia, Wyoming, New York, Utah, Pennsylvania, Ontario, California, Colorado, Tennessee, Texas.) And they come prepared for the long haul—with lawn chairs, ice chests, thousand-dollar binoculars, tripod-mounted spotting scopes and telephoto camera lenses like howitzers—and are polite, friendly and happily patient. Many wrote letters, gave money or time or otherwise helped effect the wolf restoration, and are here to cash in their investment.

In the afternoon, Caroline and I treat ourselves to a longish hike up Slough Creek, which naturally provokes a ferocious rainstorm. The high point of the excursion comes just after the rain, when a lone coyote comes streaking out of the trees and zigzagging down through First Meadow toward us. Right behind is an elk cow, dogging the terrified canid like a rodeo calf-roper. Soon another cow takes the baton and the first cow returns to the trees and, no doubt, to her calf. Some you win, some you lose.

The evening watch reveals a depressing lack of violent death.

∞

Another day in paradise. As soon as we hit the valley this morning we learn that the Crystal Creek pack has just tried to dig out a coyote den, apparently going for the pups within. Rick, Debbie and Jason, all of whom were in the right place at the right time to witness the action, describe it as a "free-for-all," with wolves chasing coyotes, coyotes and wolves chasing elk, elk chasing coyotes, and wolves digging furiously at the den entrance. At one point, a grizzly appeared on the hill above, surveyed the scene below, shook its head and left.

Such unkind behavior by the wolves toward their smaller canid cousins is almost certainly motivated by territoriality. A hankering for coyote flesh clearly wasn't their goal, since the one pup they apparently managed to extract from the deep dark hole was later found dead (from a bite to the head) but uneaten.

When the wolves were good and gone, the coyote parents returned and attempted to lead their two surviving pups across a foot bridge over the tumescent Lamar River and out of immediate harm's way; one followed, but the other pup refused to cross the bridge and was abandoned.

So it goes in the real world.

Across the remainder of the day we see two wolves and another grizzly, and trail a hard-working coyote pair for half a mile as they hunt rodents, scent-marking as they go.

∾

No end to the interesting characters you encounter on the Yellowstone Death Watch circuit.

Like Bob Crabtree. This quiet, friendly, bearded Ph.D. biologist heads the private, nonprofit research foundation Yellowstone Ecosystem Studies (Y.E.S.) and is the official Yellowstone coyote researcher. I've been hearing about him since we arrived, and now, at a roadside pullout, we finally meet.

What I know already is that Y.E.S. recently completed a six-year initial "pre-wolf" phase of a long-term field study of wolf impacts, including especially interactions between the park's big predators, and is now embarked on the second, "with wolves," leg of the study. After introducing myself, I ask Crabtree one sweeping question: What effects will the reintroduction of wolves likely have on Yellowstone's other large predators and their prey?

"Well," says Crabtree, fingering his whiskers thoughtfully, "let's start with some background. The six-year study we've just completed was in itself the most intensive and long-term coyote field research project ever undertaken, and we're only half done. The second part of the study will directly address your question by looking at the effects wolves will have on other predators and their prey. Obvious areas of inquiry include how many elk the wolves kill annually and which of the four large predators—bears, wolves, coyotes and mountain lions—will dominate. But we'll be studying more subtle effects as well, such as disease, prey behavior and movements in winter, and trickle-down impacts on smaller carnivores and the small-mammal prey base.

"That said and without doubt, the predators most affected by the wolves will be coyotes. Coyotes kill a lot of elk, especially calves. I've found the skeletons of as many as six elk calves at a single den. And these are just the ones they carry home. When you consider that a coyote pack changes dens two to four times during a denning season, you begin to get the picture.

"In a three-year study conducted by former National Park Service researcher Francis Singer, elk calves were radio-collared and researchers rushed right in as soon as they got a mortality signal. What they found was that equal numbers of calves were being killed by coyotes and grizzlies ... a big surprise.

"Coyotes have two primary methods of hunting elk calves. Most commonly, a pack will locate a cow with a calf, then split up, with most of the pack trying to distract the cow. Meanwhile, the remain-

ing coyotes go in and do the calf. I call the second technique 'sneak
around in the grass and lie low'; it's very catlike in that usually a lone
coyote tries to slip in close and spring on an unwary calf, killing it fast
and clean with a bite to the throat, holding on until it suffocates.

"Of course, clean kills aren't always possible, especially when
predators as small as coyotes go after prey as big as an adult elk or
deer. When necessary, coyotes will chase and harass a prey animal,
calf or adult, nipping at it until it weakens and goes down. We've seen
many cases of coyotes killing adult elk this way, most often in winter.
Elk rarely run in deep snow, but stand their ground and try to defend
themselves with their hooves. If the animal is strong, the coyotes
soon give up. But if an elk is old or sick or otherwise weak and vulnerable, the coyotes will keep chipping away at it with quick twisting
bites, trying to cause as much bleeding as they can, wearing the prey
down until it's safe to go in for the kill. They're incredibly patient
hunters; I know of one instance where coyotes held a deer in water
for five days to weaken it."

Here I feel compelled to interrupt with a pressing interrogative:
What does Dr. Crabtree tell people who witness such disturbing acts
of predation and are repulsed by them, feeling sympathy for the prey
and hatred for the predators—the "Bambi effect"?

"I tell them that predators have to eat too. They're evolved to kill
live prey, so that's what they do. Carnivores need meat in order to
survive and raise their young, and the only way they have of getting
it is to kill and scavenge. The anthropomorphic concept of 'cruelty'
simply doesn't apply to predators.

"Anyhow, after coyotes, the second greatest impact of the wolves
will probably be on grizzlies. Some people think the wolves will have
a negative net effect on bears by pushing them off kills, and evidence
certainly exists to indicate that a full pack of *hungry* wolves is capable of doing just that. Up in Canada, Paul Pacquet has recorded
eleven cases of lone grizzlies competing with wolves for a freshly
killed carcass, and in each case the wolves won.

"Even so, here in Yellowstone, with our abundance of elk, I think grizzlies will benefit from wolf kills. Already we've had four documented instances of grizzlies pushing wolves off kills. In every case, though, the wolves had already fed and apparently relinquished the left-overs to the bears without serious resistance. You never know; some incredible things happen when predators compete for a meal.

"For example: In his seven-year study of Yellowstone mountain lions, Kerry Murphy of the Hornocker Wildlife Research Institute documented several cases of coyotes knocking lions off their kills. Conversely, more than a dozen coyotes are known to have been killed by lions—generally when a lone dog attempts to scavenge a meal from a carcass being guarded by a lion.

"In all such instances, two primary variables determine the outcome of predator interactions at kill sites: total muscle mass, and satiation; who's the strongest—by numbers or size—and who's the hungriest?

"Mountain lions and bears are solitary predators, while wolves and coyotes most often hunt in packs. So when you have a confrontation between predators over a kill, it's not as simple as the largest, the grizzly, always being dominant, the wolf next and so on. We have one case here in the park where researchers Steve and Marilyn French watched a pack of coyotes push a big boar grizzly off its kill; the coyotes—the dominant male in particular—would flash in and nip at the bear's butt then dart away, gradually wearing down the grizzly's resolve to defend a carcass on which it had already had a good feed. Had the bear been hungrier, and therefore more motivated, the outcome would likely have been different.

"All of that notwithstanding, a determined wolf pack will almost always dominate other predators, even grizzlies, in a conflict over a kill.

"Concerning wolves versus coyotes—what we saw this morning, where wolves forced coyotes to abandon a den of pups, was five wolves against four coyotes. In another recent case, five coyotes chased off two wolves. Who wins in a conflict between wild canids is generally determined by mutual assessment: How many coyotes versus how many wolves? And how big and healthy are the animals on each team? We're seeing a lot more chasing, bluffing and posturing than actual fighting.

"As to what effects the wolves may have on local elk—I think we'll see only a slight reduction in elk numbers due to direct wolf predation, probably no more than 10 percent. This, in turn, could stimulate calf production, offsetting the predation.

"Another important effect may be an increased predator wariness among the elk; we've seen signs that wapiti are already discriminating between coyotes and wolves. This could lead to increased energy costs for the ungulates—more time spent watching for predators and less time spent feeding—which could lead to increased elk winterkill. Which, in turn, would mean more carcasses for all kinds of scavengers each spring.

"Also, we might see wolves pushing elk out of some prime foraging areas, spreading them more evenly across the range, with a net positive result for the ecosystem. It would be great, for instance, if the wolves could keep elk from ganging up in fragile riparian areas.

"It's important to remember that wolves divide into packs and spread themselves out broadly and more or less evenly over their available hunting territory. Here on the Northern Range, we have nearly twenty thousand elk and probably will never have more than fifty wolves divided into five or six packs. Obviously, that number of wolves will never be a threat to the elk population.

"And too, the wolves can be expected to more than offset their own kills by reducing coyote predation. Wolves weigh about three times more than coyotes—ninety pounds versus thirty pounds on the average. But the wolf's territory is ten to twelve times larger than the coyote's. What this says is that the total canid biomass in a situation with all coyotes and no wolves is four times greater than with all wolves and no coyotes.

"Right now, coyotes are probably two to three times more numerous than they were before wolves were exterminated from the park, making them the dominant predators of ungulates in the ecosystem. My prediction is that we'll see up to a two-thirds reduction in coyote numbers in areas where wolves colonize.

"What I expect to see as the end result of wolf reintroduction is (1) a drastic reduction in coyotes, probably by around half, (2) observable changes in ungulate behavior, (3) increased numbers of coyote prey species—everything from elk down to voles and mice—which, in turn, will provide more prey for other predators, and (4) things shaking down so that each of the four dominant large-predator species will be killing similar numbers of elk, democratizing predation, with the result that quality of the elk herds will increase significantly while quantity drops very little."

ᘓ

Morning again, which we celebrate by watching from the Cache Creek pullout as three grizzlies goof around on a distant hillside (one of them mostly just sits and plays with its toes), and five adult wolves—two black, three gray—munch on rosy chunks of an elk calf they've just killed and divvied up.

When the morning action slows, we join Debbie and Jason for a long bushwhack hike that takes us over a high ridge and out of sight of the road, into the hidden realm of grizzly and wolf.

In early afternoon, as we approach an open bench with a piano-sized rock outcrop at its center, Jason points and says "That's exactly the kind of place elk like to hide their calves." No sooner spoken than I almost trod upon a white-spotted sorrel lump curled unmoving against a downed tree near that very boulder. "Case closed," says a grinning Jason. I snap a few quick pictures and we move on.

Across the next several hours we discover a second cataleptic calf and the skeletal remains, still articulated, of several adult elk, winterkills devoured in recent weeks by scavengers, including especially bears. But no up-close, uptight griz encounters, and fine by us.

Late in the evening, after returning to our vehicles for dinner, then lugging our observer accouterments to a low promontory near a stinking calcium-carbonate anthill called Soda Butte, Jason promptly lays glass on a sow grizzly and two big cubs romping helter-skelter through a sage flat across the valley, apparently trying to frighten any wapiti waifs hidden thereabouts into flight. By the time I get my scope aimed and focused, the bears have retreated into an adjacent aspen grove and are conducting a slow search throughout, three silent ghosts gliding amongst the white-barked trunks.

At sunset, a lone coyote appears on a knoll close above us, raises his pointy muzzle in a picture-perfect "Santa Fe style" pose and yodels his joy. I can't help but howl back, which earns me a scowl from Jason, my second of the day. (The first came when I failed to step over an ant bed while we were hiking, causing momentary chaos in the pismire community. When Jason, by way of chastising me, praised ants as "tireless workers," I said that's precisely why I detest them. "You're puttin' me on!" was Jason's incredulous response. I just smiled.)

Meanwhile, on naked stone cliffs to the east, a bachelor band of six bighorn rams attend to their dizzying business as usual, their primary predator being gravity.

ॐ

Comes the weekend, and with it our Missoula friends Dan, Anita and baby Liza Crockett. Dan and Anita—avid hunters, fly fishers and conservationists as well as superb wild-game chefs—volunteer to prepare dinner *alfresco* at the Lamar picnic area: hibachi-smoked mallard, fresh veggies and herbed spuds. More grateful than helpful, I kick back in my folding chair, a tumbler of Dickel and water in one hand, Zeiss binocs in the other, hoping for the return of that subadult griz pair who've been frequenting the aspens just across the river in recent days.

After being told there's nothing she can do to help with dinner, Caroline sets about updating her wildflower trip list: spring beauty, shooting star, fairy slipper orchid, wild strawberry, wild parsley, biscuitroot, balsamroot, pasqueflower, penstemmon, phlox, clematis, larkspur, vaseflower, violet, Indian paintbrush, mountain bluebell, forget-me-not and … "I forget what else."

For a full lazy hour we sit and sip and watch and listen as a thousand wapiti and hundreds of bison graze bucolically on the sprawling river plain … as a litter of fat coyote pups romp just outside their den on a sage slope across the road … as geese honk, meadowlarks whistle and cow elk bugle anomalously (only bull elk are "supposed" to bugle, and then only during the fall rut) … as a raft of white pelicans float in elegant silence down the oxbowed river and a pair of pterodactyl-like sandhill cranes blare out their prehistoric exclamations of *garooo-a, krooo-ooo* … as a light of impossible beauty invests the evening with magic.

This place, this broad pristine valley in the northeast corner of our oldest national park, is often referred to as the American Serengeti, and rightly so. But on this preternaturally sublime evening, even that is insufficient praise; it's as if we've been transported back to the Pleistocene … back to Eden.

"Duck's done," quacks lovely little Liza.

We rise and gingerly circumnavigate several tons of churlish bison on our way to nature's table.

∾

So it goes. And come Monday afternoon, the Crocketts go too, back to the antlike "civilized" world of work and worry.

Across our fleeting week here, we've been happily tormented by scores of excited reports recounting all we've missed. For our part, through long hours of watching and miles of relaxed hiking, we've seen a total of "only" eight wolves (doing what wolves do: catnapping, hunting, eating, scent-marking, playing, rolling in bison dung) and eight grizzlies—including most recently a big cinnamon bruin Caroline spotted near the campground road carrying off a just-killed elk calf. I missed that action, distracted by the frantic antics of the slain tike's mother.

So and sadly, it's our last evening here and we're out cruising for trouble. When we spot a throng of watchers lined out on a sage flat just east of Lamar Canyon, I park the truck and we leap out and scamper up the hill to see what gives. What we find is a massive blond grizzly with chocolate legs and muzzle munching on an inert elk calf in a sage pocket two hundred yards from the road—as close as you ever want to get to a bear on a kill. With full equipage, we hurry to join our fellow blood-and-guts voyeurs.

As we're approaching, a scowling man wearing a bulging khaki photo vest and carrying a camera dwarfed by a bazooka lens goes stomping away, red-faced and mumbling incoherently.

"What's with him?" I ask the young man I've just moved in next to.

"Mr. Jerk there?" says he, smiling and nodding his chin toward the departing photographer. "Showed up an hour ago and started bragging that he's trying to graduate from real estate brochures to professional wildlife photography; thinks he has to be close enough to count eyelashes to get pictures that will sell. Hi, I'm Tim."

"I'm Dave and this is Caroline. He wanted to get closer? With a lens like *that?* Had to be at least a five hundred."

"Eight," says Tim's pal, who introduces himself as Wayne, at which several other nearby watchers—serious folk who obviously don't suffer fools or bombastic wannabes gladly—erupt in a chorus of chuckles.

When I ask why Mr. Jerk left in such a huff, Wayne shrugs and grins shyly. "Who knows? Last thing he said to me was, 'Wonder what would happen if I tried to get closer to the bear?'"

"And the last thing you said to him," Tim reminds Wayne, "was, 'I'll trip you.'"

More laughter. Then the matter and the man are forgotten.

Short-haired Tim and long-haired Wayne, I soon learn, are first-timers up from "Salt Lick City." Wayne has just bagged a master's degree in wildlife biology, and Tim is a small-business owner. "In the fall," Wayne explains, "we're hunters. The rest of the year, we're watchers."

My kind of folk.

"We read about this in last Sunday's paper," says Tim, "about the bears and wolves and elk and all, and decided to come see it for ourselves. We left Salt Lick at daylight Wednesday and got here in time to see two wolves that same evening and a grizzly bear the next morning. Pretty amazing, eh?"

Eh, indeed. As is the sight before us now. This gorgeous big bear has obviously been working on the elk for some time, since little remains but hide and bones, which tattered bundle she periodically picks up and shakes like a terrier with a toy. As the evening unfolds, the bear alternately gnaws, plays with and naps on the deflated calf—even as the mother elk stands silhouetted on the ridge directly above, watching, as if in hopes her babe will spring back to life and escape.

When the biggest coyote I've ever seen comes dodging in to try and cadge a piece of the action, the groggy, overstuffed bear rouses long enough to take one somnambulant swipe at the intruder, then yawns and returns to her nap. The big dog is persistent and eventually succeeds in pilfering a crimson morsel, with which it lopes jauntily away.

Storm clouds have threatened rain all afternoon, but now they part, painting a brief brilliant rainbow across the valley to our backs. When the watchers turn away en masse to admire the vivid scene, the sow rises on her haunches and stares intently, as if she feels slighted by our sudden collective lapse of interest. Or maybe she too is enjoying the show.

Now, jogging up from the road, a Japanese woman spots the bear and turns to her American companion sitting in their idling car. "Quick!" she yells. "Come here! Bring the camera! It's a bear! He's eating! How *cute!*"

While all of this has been going down—the jabber, the joking, the exchange of watcher war stories, the rainbow, the comings and goings of Tourons—a middle-aged man a few heads down the line, bald as a baby, hatless and sunburned, has spent as much time watching the watchers as he has the bear, yet hasn't cracked a smile or uttered a word. I've been eyeing his big black bazooka, a twin to the one that departed with Mr. Jerk, comparing it jealously to my own puny little three hundred. Curious and covetous, I grab my camera and stroll on over.

"Hi," I venture.

Silence. The man appears suspicious (and rightly so).

"Say," I say, "I was wondering … how much would you charge to let me put my camera on your lens and bang off a few quick shots of the bear?"

With a devilish grin and a heavy German accent, both of which take me by surprise, the silent man speaks: "How much are you willing to *pay?*"

Ouch.

Thus touchéd, I dump photography in favor of international diplomacy. "Why," I ask, sincere now, "would you spend thousands of marks to come all the way from Germany just to watch wild animals eating one another?"

"Ha!" says he, serious and frowning again. "Because we Europeans weren't far-seeing enough to preserve anything like this." He sweeps the verdant horizon with a hairy arm, pausing at the bear. "We took it all for our own use and profit—the wilderness, the wildlife, the *wild*ness—and impoverished our continent, and ourselves, in the doing. There's no place else like this left anywhere in the temperate world outside Denali, especially now that the wolves are back. I follow international politics and I worry at the way things are going here in the States; I came to see this place and these animals before you Americans make the same mistake we did."

Warming to this dour, frank fellow, my good humor returning, I affect a conspiratorial expression and ask: "Have you gotten to see a bear or a wolf actually making a kill yet?"

"Not yet."

I step closer and lower my voice to a whisper, like someone offering a hot tip at the track. "Well," I advise with a wink and a nod, "keep watching. Because I'll guarantee ya, the first time you see it, you'll get a rush that'll surpass anything in your entire pharmaceutical history."

17

Good Times in the Owyhee Badlands

FOR YEARS I'D HEARD stories of a lonesome place in the interior West where rivers run clear in deep desert canyons and almost nobody ever goes. But par for my course, I couldn't quite recall the name of the place ... something vaguely Polynesian, maybe. So I phoned my professional adventurer friend Tim. It's a good bet that anyplace you or I might ever want to go, he's already been there and will recall it in photographic detail.

"Tim," I said, getting right to it (my nickel), "I'm trying to remember the name of this place: high desert in Idaho, or Oregon maybe; serious boonies, scenic canyons, odd name."

"That would be the Owyhee badlands, out where Nevada, Idaho and Oregon meet. High semi-desert sagebrush steppes and plateaus, average elevation around forty-five hundred feet. The Owyhee River heads in northern Nevada and flows northwest into Oregon, where it's joined by the Middle and North forks out of Idaho; drains about eight thousand square miles.

"It's the river canyons—eroded in places as deep as twelve hundred feet into volcanic basalt, rhyolite and tuff—that make Owyhee country special. In fact, it's the lower forty-eight's most remote and least known whitewater river system, with most of its length proposed for National Wild and Scenic River status and just one paved road crossing it in Oregon, none in Idaho. During the spring run-off it's a maelstrom of Class IV and V rapids, with very few places where you can climb up out of the canyons should something go wrong. It's a waterworld kind of desert."

"O-whatey?"

"*O-Y-He.* Cowboy bastardization of Hawaii. Back in the 1830s, three immigrant Hawaiian fur trappers disappeared in there. The canyons ate them. Or maybe the Indians did. Cold in winter, hot in summer. When do you plan to go?"

"Early July."

"May and June are better."

"It's July or never."

"You'll need a high-clearance vehicle, four-by-four if it rains. Carry extra gas and water, a water filter, good maps and a compass. No trails, all bushwhacking. Have fun."

I hate widely traveled people with flawless memories.

Next I phoned a couple of folks in Idaho I'd been tipped were experienced Owyhee hikers, then applied their advice to the only maps I could come up with on such short notice—a Bureau of Land Management 1:100,000 "surface mining management status" planimetric cluttered with bureaucrapic trivia and devoid of even such basics as contours, and an Idaho Department of Transportation sheet of the same scale with contours at gaping twenty-meter intervals.

Perusing the maps, it quickly became evident that the Owyhee badlands are so expansive that investing the meagre week I had at my disposal in a single marathon hike into one little corner would be, well … risky. Instead, I opted to make this premiere trip a hop-scotch exploration comprising three shorter, though not short hikes. It would mean a little more time spent driving and a little less hiking, but it would net a far better sense of the whole enchilada. For proven pleasant company, I invited good old Branson Reynolds.

ॐ

And so it happened, two butt-numbing days ago, that Branson and I fled condo-infested, Californicated Colorado and motored north-west, arriving here—well, just now—at the Middle Fork Owyhee River twenty-some miles beyond the Shoshone-Paiute village of Owyhee, Nevada, on the Duck Valley Indian Reservation (popula-tion: twelve hundred). A few miles more of driving, off-pavement now, and my two-bit maps intimate that we've left the reservation and back-doored into Idaho.

At road's end, we unfold our crumpled bods from my tuna-can pickup and stroll over to the rim of the canyon, a great gaping gash in an otherwise ho-hum sage plain. Viewed in cross-section, the canyon here is like a wine glass, with the gently sloping upper half forming the cup and the narrow, vertical-walled river gorge the stem. The cliff walls are gray-brown lava brightened by multi-colored lichen and shotgunned through with shallow caves.

From up here on the edge of the outer rim, the way down to the lip of the inner gorge is a steep rocky slope grown high in cheatgrass, thistle and other livestock-imported aliens that have all but crowded out the native flora. Mummified cow pies foul the landscape every-where. A most unpleasant obstacle course, withal, neither attractive nor inviting. Hardly a place any sensible hiker would ever choose to hike. Good; we likes our privacy.

Branson and I return to the truck for our packs, vowing to spend the night on some cool streamside beach far below—assuming we can find a way down. Since we're heading into a prolonged July Fourth weekend, the possibility of encountering other hikers, even way out here, is real. My maps, such as they are, hint at a couple of possible tourist attractions north a ways—a scenic, serpentine sec-tion of canyon called the Meanders and, a ways north of that, an oxbow lake dubbed the Tules. We head south.

◆

It's midafternoon and furnace-hot when we begin our descent into the upper canyon. At the inner rim we creep to the precipitous edge, peek over and see, way down, a tranquillity of pools the color of weak tea interspersed with small falls and shallow riffles. A month or two ago it would have been a roaring, foaming turmoil of whitewater down there. But the run-off has all run off, and the stream now is placid.

I haul out my binoculars and spot several small fish in a big pool directly below us, lipping at the mirrored surface for their winged lunch of *baetis* and such. In adjacent shallow water over a sunny sandbar basks a huge torpedo of a fish, two feet or longer, its species unknowable from here.

Boulders big as Buicks litter the river and its beaches, the latter grown florid with what appear (through binoculars) to be sego lilies, wild rose and osiers; confirming the latter, the uric scent of desert willow rises on midday thermals.

Between us and the river stretches an airy feathered void darting with swifts and swallows, swooping with red-tailed hawks and unknown falcons, soaring with eagles and vultures and cavorting with killdeer.

We slouch onward through the heat, stepping now and again to the edge to peer into the dizzying depth, but never finding a way down other than free-fall. Every now and again the breeze dies and when it does, gnats and deerflies become our pestiferous companions. We walk when we can and lava-hop when we must. We're both wearing shorts and low-topped boots, and our socks bristle with cheatgrass thistles. We'd been warned to wear long pants and high-topped leather boots to this cow-burnt wasteland, but didn't. Dumb and dumber.

As evening approaches, we grudgingly admit defeat, having neither the time nor the skills necessary to descend to the river anywhere along here. Thus, we are doomed to bivouac tonight halfway down, on the inner rim, with only what water we're carrying. Still, it

could be worse. The view to the horizon all around is distant and
devoid of any sign of man. (Or, notes bachelor Branson, "wo-man.")
Sunset is a glorious crimson flare in the west. Night folds in and coyotes yodel all around.

ᐁ

With daylight, having had enough of cheatgrass, bugs and lava-hot
hiking through what resembles an abandoned feedlot, we hump and
grump back up to the truck and embark on a long, semiboring drive
back through the Duck Valley rez—a clean, well-watered place compared to the surrounding BLM wasteland—and up Idaho Highways
51 and 78 to Grand View (hyperbole), where we lurch around for a
while, semilost, stumbling at last onto the Owyhee Uplands National
Back Country Byway, known locally as Mud Flat Road.

This gravelly ranchway extends 103 miles from Grand View, Idaho,
to Jordan Valley, Oregon, more or less splitting the distance between
the Middle and North forks of the river. It is, as the late great Supreme
Court Justice William O. Douglas would have it, a dagger placed in the
heart of wilderness. Still, it's here, so we use it. (Morality these days
gets so damn complicated.)

The country is lower here, a varied topography of bumpy sage
plains watered by occasional small creeks. It's also graced with a
more vibrant and varied flora. The flowering apogee of spring is long
past, yet we identify (or guess at) sego lily, showy daisy, bladderpod,
lupine, phlox, bitterroot, bitterbrush, rabbitbrush, Indian paintbrush, greasewood, purple aster, Hooker's onion, a stunning array of
LYFs (little yellow flowers) and a blue-green sea of sage. Clusters of
mountain mahogany whisker the hilltops, shrubby western junipers
freckle the slopes and an occasional lime-green grove of quaking
aspen provides flickering shade for indolent lounging wads of
hooved hamburgers.

This night we bivouac along a brief sideroad amongst swarms, hordes, gaggles, batches of bluebirds. A prolonged scarlet sunset backlights one lonely mountain mahogany, lending it briefly the grace of an African baobab (the tree where Man was born).

Thunder rumbles and lightning flashes, bullying us into erecting the tent—then no rain comes. Tomorrow, we'll launch a backpack exploration of the intertwined Camel/Camas/Pole creek drainages in the midst of a BLM Wilderness Study Area and proposed Air Force bombing range.

~

An hour after sunrise, we abandon the relative security of Mud Flat Road (itself one of the most remote byways in America), lock into four-by-four and go bumping out across an overgrazed sage flat on a two-track torture trail that twists and climbs slowly onto a juniper-clad mesa. Up here it's less abused by livestock, with less noxious flora and more wildflowers; penstemon and wild onion predominate. One lovely mule deer doe watches us pass, her mouth full of cud, and when we descend into a broad open basin a dozen pronghorns take flight, sprinting off with their definitive, ground-gobbling stride, graceful as soaring birds.

Now we're getting somewhere.

Eventually we reach what my so-called maps hint might be a promising trailhead—minus any trail—from which to launch our investigation of Pole Creek canyon and its tributaries. Up one of these, I've been advised, waits a haunting panel of prehistoric petroglyphs.

Humans have occupied this region for more than twelve thousand years. What might it have been like to live here back then? Your daily work would have consisted mostly of hunting mammoths and other massive Pleistocene mammals, armed only with clubs and stone-tipped spears. No school to attend, no taxes to pay, no progressive mindset to screw up everything, no pollution to suffer, no land whores driving Mercedes, no politics or politicians. Real Garden of Eden stuff; the good *old* days.

We lunch in the shade of a massive ancient juniper on a knoll with a view, then saddle up (being our own pack animals) and lumber off in search of a way down into what we *think* is Pole Creek canyon, here little more than a hundred feet deep. We soon find that way and side-step down, the going made interesting by a litter of egg-sized geodes that roll like ball-bearings from beneath our boots.

We make it to the bottom unbruised and are rewarded by a riparian paradise unsullied, at least so far this summer, by cows or woolly maggots. The creek runs clear and slow, its clean sand beaches verdant with willow osiers, reeds, sedges and a scattering of sego lilies, Indian paintbrush and other dryland wildflowers. Having come prepared (for once), we zip the legs off our convertible pants, trade boots for sandals, unbuckle the hip belts of our packs (for safety, you know) and otherwise prepare for a splashing good time.

While we're about these little chores, a lone eagle—its feathers a lustrous golden-brown, its wingspan as broad as I am tall—appears overhead, slicing effortlessly into a stiff canyon-rim wind. A hundred feet above us, she performs a graceful aileron roll then jets back down-canyon with big yellow beak agape, savoring the flavor of wind, the taste of freedom. Paranoid public-lands, public-welfare sheep ranchers, typically over-reacting to the occasional loss of a lamb or two, shoot and poison these magnificent creatures at every opportunity. And frequently, in blatant disregard of its own laws, the government helps. At your expense and mine.

The eagle is not alone. The sky within and above the canyon swarms with a stunning array of ascended dinosaurs: swallows, swifts, robins, the prairie falcons and American kestrels who rip the smaller birds wing from bod and devour them bloody hot, plus one sinister undertaker buzzard—the official Owyhee badlands bird.

I love desert stream hiking—sloshing knee-deep through a compatible coalescence of fire and water—and the going here is cool and easy, though occasionally slick with moss.

Hours pass, if not so many miles, and on a pebbled beach beneath a shady alcove we splash ashore for a break. While I peel and devour an orange, Branson photographs a lichen-stained (lime, orange, lemon) canyon wall across the way. I like lichen—a tough and tenacious life form with minimal needs. Another local survivor, though much more delicate and demanding in its habitat needs, is the California desert bighorn, small bands of which haunt these remote rugged canyons, transplanted here in the 1960s and rarely seen since. Certainly not today, by us, so far.

A lazy afternoon breeze sighs through the willows. Desert water tinkles in the creek. A female canyon wren, the quintessential desert songstress, gushes out her flutelike ode to joy, then flits into the alcove and perches on the cribriform ceiling, upside down, a meaty bug squirming in her spearlike beak. I can't see her chicks back in their lava-cave nest, but their frenetic squabbling for the insect morsel animates the alcove with a cacophony of echoes.

More water-walking. More desert sights, sounds, smells.

The afternoon has cooled to early evening when we emerge from our day's wading all wrinkle-skinned, bummed at not having found the petroglyphs but smiling just the same.

We sit down, zip our legs on, boot-up and wriggle up through a narrow cut in the cliff to the sage plain above. Rubbernecking, we spot a distant junipered mesa and unanimously elect it our night's goal. Toward that end we walk, more or less aimlessly, unrestricted by any trail, until we come to a creek too small to show on my magnificent maps. The little seep meanders more or less mesaward, so we follow its cool green trace, hoping to encounter wildlife come to water.

Soon, lying low in the glaring western distance, we spot two dark rectangular forms. What the hey? *Buildings* in a Wilderness Study Area? It's our duty to investigate.

What we find are two fourteen-square-foot hewn-log cabins, cobby and ramshackle. After a cautious perusal for scorpions and rattlers—of whose abundance in Owyhee country much is made, though we've yet to encounter either—we venture into the nearest shack and find there a splintered plank floor, the rusted remains of an iron cookstove, stumps for stools, cobwebs, rodent turds.

The second cabin, even more primitive and likely older, has only a dusty dirt floor and a collapsed stone fireplace. Both buildings retain remnants of mud chinking in their walls and sport sod roofs bristling with native bunchgrass two feet high.

Who? When? Why?

If Owyhee country is arguably the most remote area in the lower forty-eight today, what must it have been like here more than a century ago? As a white settler, the only people you'd be likely to see for months on end would be churlish Indians whose land you were stealing. A crushingly lonely, physically brutal, potentially hair-raising existence. The *real* Old West.

Treading lightly among scarlet gilia, pastel penstemon, yellow-eyed daisy, pumpkin-orange globe mallow and ubiquitous wild onions (I snatch and gobble handfuls of the umbellate cream-and-lavender Hooker's: *muy picante!*), we circumnavigate the cabins and see where coyotes have tunneled beneath.

Ironically, tragically and typically, these priceless historic relics will become bombing targets if the Air Force and a Good Old Boy (and in this instance, Girl) conspiracy of "state's rights," "wise use" Idaho politicians and their profiteering corporate rancher pals get their way. That "way" being a U.S. Air Force composite tactical warfare bombing range comprising three distinct firing and bombing zones, an electronic combat range, plus copious dropping of flares and chaff, low-level flights throughout and supersonic "boomer" runs above ten thousand feet. While "only" twenty-five thousand acres are targeted as actual impact zones, the low-level flights and barrage of sonic and explosive booms would torture and cripple some three million acres of mostly de facto wilderness. Those ancient petroglyphs we failed to find today and these landmark cabins would become a different kind of history entirely. The reticent and nervous California bighorns would be rendered impotent and, ultimately, gone.

And more, all of it bad.

Happily, the acute threat has been temporarily diffused through the hard-fought efforts of concerned local activists, including especially the Shoshone-Paiute Indian Tribe and the Committee for Idaho's High Desert. But like the wilderness Terminators they are, the bad guys (including especially one very bad girl) have vowed, "We'll be back."

We briefly consider spending the night in this miniature ghost town, but opt to leave the spirits of Owyhee's past, and the resident coyotes, to their lonely peace. Filled with nostalgia for a time we never knew, we turn and walk away.

ॐ

There's plenty of evening left in this summer day when we finally reach our room for the night: a junipered mesa with a wrap-around view, cooling breezes, abundant firewood and an uncowed seep spring from which to rehydrate our desiccated corpses.

Exhausted, we make our camp—sleeping bags rolled out on ground cloths—amongst some of the most ancient and massive western junipers extant. I'm six feet flat and Branson two inches over, and we can't even come close to joining hands around their massive shaggy trunks. Why haven't these hefty suckers been logged? Such a valuable "resource" going to "waste."

After a feast of dehydrated noodles, crackers and water, feeling rested but talked-out for the nonce, we go our separate ways. Branson wanders off to take pictures, while I just wander.

Strolling (you could say care-less-ly) through a patchwork of onion-scented meadows and juniper-flavored woods at the edge of night, I'm suddenly bushwhacked by an inexplicable sense of well-being. What's going on? I stop and stand in silence, smiling like the happy idiot I am, and eavesdrop on the evening chatter of blue-birds, nighthawks, robins and an anonymous assortment of little gray singers: lovely wild voices twittering amongst the brushy trees.

In full darkness I trail the scent of juniper smoke back to camp— Branson has already returned—and retire to the haunting calls of poorwills, the maniacal music of coyotes.

∾

On the road again.

What remains of the Mud Flat thruway carries us eventually to the Mormonesque ranching village of Jordan Valley, Oregon; "Dog Town" back in its gold-boom days, but today a clean, sun-lighted place.

We stop for water, gas and gas (a cafe lunch of chicken-fried chicken and Basque beans). Replenished, we motor west on Oregon 95, a pleas-ant little blacktop byway, then dodge off onto another dusty ranch road. Twenty minutes along this rutted rural route we come to the official BLM Owyhee Canyon (Middle Fork) overlook.

Your standard awe-inspiring western vista, this. The canyon here is reminiscent of the Rio Grande Gorge north of Taos—yawning wide, dizzying deep (a thousand feet or more) and overtly foreboding. Its rusted lava cliffs are splashed orange and lime with living lichen. Talus scree rests at ten million angles of repose. Green-trimmed beaches border a rushing river so distant that its roar rises to us as a mere faint whisper. Meanwhile and above it all, hard-edged silver clouds sail in a cobalt sky.

Past the overlook, the ranch road gradually deteriorates to reveal its 1860s stage trail origins. An hour off the blacktop, we come to a sudden severe drop, beyond and below which waits the Three Forks of the Owyhee—at long hot last.

I bang old Betsy into four-wheel/low and brake cautiously downward, arriving eventually riverside. Here the BLM has placed a stinking Port-a-Potty near a tiny ancient log cabin, perhaps a relic of Camp Winthrop, a hard-luck 1860s army outpost. I imagine back 130 years to when this very spot was a bullet-riddled battleground, not once but many times, between the U.S. Cavalry and American Indians. To wit, from *Owyhee Trails*, by Mike Hanley:

> At last [the cavalry] found the warriors, about 500 strong, at Three Forks and the Indians drove the troops off, costing the Army four men, their artillery tents, and some provisions. The troopers dug in on the west bank, with the tribesmen across the way. ... [After a while] the troopers tried to get the howitzer over the river, but the raft made of driftwood capsized in the rush of water and the gun went to the bottom. One of the men on the raft ... mistakenly reached the enemy bank. The hostiles roped him around the neck and dragged him through the brush.

Good on the "hostiles." (Which is not to say shame on that poor trooper, who likely didn't want to be there; but it *is* nice to see the Indians win one occasionally.)

We de-truck and hurry down to the river, which we find cool and clear and inviting but way too deep to wade. Were we on the far bank—over there where the "bad guys" once hunkered down to harass the "friendlies"—our night's goal would be but an easy hour's stroll along a slender strand of willowed beach through a narrow, vertical-walled canyon. Not far beyond that shady portal, I hear tell, a geothermally warmed creek fills a deep stone pool perched on a narrow ledge, then overflows in a gentle cascade to the river forty feet below.

A miracle in the desert. One you can soak in.

But we are here, not over there, and rather than build a driftwood raft on which to float, and likely capsize, cavalry-style, we opt for a rock-'n-roll stretch of stage trail that climbs and switchbacks and plummets to a historic river crossing near the warm pool and falls. Compared to the brief canyon hike (were we on the other side), this way is long, hot, steep, dusty and dry. But it gets us there.

Here.

Where we want to be at last. We immediately erect the tent—not against bugs or weather, but as a territorial marker should interlopers appear. (With high-clearance four-by or ATV and some measure of recklessness, our stagecoach "hiking" trail could be, and obviously has been, driven.)

Camp set, we strip down and splash into the chilly river, wading across and fighting through a screen of tules to the base of the falls, where we stand with arms spread like crucified thieves and let the eighty-degree flood scour us clean of a week's trail grime (if not a life-time of sin). Long languorous minutes later, our purgative showers completed, we scramble up a mossy rock slope to Owyhee heaven.

Local legend holds that back in the good old Depression days a CCC work crew mule-packed in here with dynamite and pick-axes to blast and chisel this unlikely stone tub into existence. If so, it doesn't show. In fact, it looks natural as can be—maybe twelve feet across at the widest and five feet deep, clear and effervescent as seltzer with a colorful stream-pebble bottom.

"Perfect," says Branson as he eases in.

The sweltering July afternoon has cooled to evening before we can bring ourselves to leave the pool. Puckered like prunes, we lizard down past the falls and wade the chilly, groin-deep Owyhee back to camp. Off in the west, a pyrotechnic sunset boils and churns in a thousand hues of orange.

As we're heating powdered soup for dinner, an aquatic hatch erupts, with swarms of tiny silk-winged mayflies (like #18 parachute Adams) emerging from the river, minuscule Ladies of the Lake rising to hover nervously around our heads.

As if an alarm has been sounded, a pair of nighthawks soon appear, diving and swooping amongst this fortuitous feast, their under-wing "windows" flashing white in the low evening light as they execute a flawless repertoire of aerobatic maneuvers—barrel and aileron rolls, high-speed dives with whooshing flares to a stall ... the whole air-show shebang—reaffirming their status as the Top Guns of the bird world.

As darkness gathers, the fish of the water join the birds of the air in the action, dimpling the river's glassy surface with their discrete feeding.

To tent.

Sometime after midnight, I'm awakened by a flurry of noisy activity over on Branson's side of our little nylon shelter. My first bleary thought is that some small animal has wandered in through the open flap, panicked and performed a double-time exit, bouncing off the gossamer tent walls en route. But when I switch on my headlamp, I see only the slow rise and fall of Branson's comatose breathing. All is silent.

Morning arrives (always a reassuring occurrence), and as I pad barefoot out to relieve my bulging bladder I spot something odd in the damp sand just outside the tent. Investigating, I find a hodge-podge of fresh coyote tracks. Reading the spoor, I interpolate that the curious canid emerged from the willows, crept toward the tent—then whirled with a spray of sand and sprinted back into the osiers. End of story. The sound that awakened me would have been his tail (or hers), whapping the tent as she (or he) fled. Must have gotten a noseful of something s/he didn't like, over there on Branson's side.

Thinking about breakfast, I glance down at my watch and realize that today is the fourth—that is, the *Fourth*—of July, the busiest, booziest and most raucous outdoor holiday of the year. And here we are—Branson, the other beasts and me—happily alone, quietly enjoying good times in the Owyhee badlands.

God bless American wilderness.

18

Footloose in the
North Cascades

A HOT-PINK SUNSET warms our first evening here in the North Cascades of Washington state. I take this as a good omen—"red sky at night," etc. It's midsummer and thermally pleasant and the bugs aren't half bad, so rather than mess with the tent, Branson and I simply toss out ground cloths and shake out our bags on top.

About midnight it starts to rain.

☙

When the urge first struck to come here, all I knew of the North Cascades, personally, was a smudge of memory dating to Labor Day 1978, registered in a blur while motoring northward through constant rain and fog during a three-day cycle sprint from Tijuana to Vancouver ("two-up," as they say, with Caroline on behind). This time around, I was determined to see the *real* Cascades, far off any blacktop, back where grizzer bears and wolves still roam (a precious imperiled few of each, at least, and no thanks to us). Back of beyond.

But where, exactly? It's a whopping big place. There are 505,000 acres in North Cascades National Park alone, another 117,000 in the Ross Lake National Recreation Area fringing down the park's northeastern border and belting west along the North Cascades Highway (Washington 20). And south from there just half a day's drive is Lake Chelan National Recreation Area with 62,000 acres more. About 93

193

percent of the combined total acreage of these three parcels is designated wildlands, known collectively as the Stephen Mather Wilderness, home to some 360 miles of maintained trails and a lifetime of
off-trail bushwhacking possibilities.

Add to this the 1,706,000 acres of the Okanogan National Forest
with its 1600 miles of trails—including the Pasayten and Lake
Chelan–Sawtooth Wilderness Areas—and you begin to sense the
magnitude of choices faced by virgin backcountry visitors. And this
not even counting the entire west slope of the Cascades, which I've
elected to leave to the locals who swarm up from the coastal mega-
lopoli of Seattle, Tacoma, Bellingham and Vancouver.

In an orgy of long-distance phone calls—to North Cascades
National Park, various Forest Service offices and the U.S. Fish and
Wildlife Service—I managed to narrow it down considerably. Perhaps
a bit too considerably. Problem was, this past winter covered the high
Cascades with far in excess of the average fifteen feet or more of snow.
(The record is something like forty-six feet.) Consequently, major
sections of the alpine Pacific Crest National Scenic Trail and most of
its network of feeder trails are not yet open this summer, and some
sections, I've been forewarned, may not open at all.

One place sure to be snow-free by mid-July, I was cheerfully
advised—and a place where, by hiking twenty miles to Cat Island
and beyond, hard below the Canadian border, we'd be well within
the recently confirmed stamping grounds of both grizzlies and
wolves—is the East Bank Ross Lake trail. I don't much care for
campground reservations, designated sites, campfire restrictions
and all the other tethers on hiking in overused areas. In fact I despise
it all. But that's progress—there are way too many of us everywhere
these days—so I acted on the official advice and reserved five nights
of blind dates.

Figuring this to be sufficient pretrip planning—why risk killing
the pleasure of discovery with an unnecessary overdose of knowl-

edge?—Branson and I hit the long hot highway north from our southern Colorado cabins.

∾

From our first night's bivouac in the Wenatchee National Forest, we motor north along the west shore of Lake Chelan. With its bottom in a glacial trough four hundred feet below sea level, this fifty-five-mile-long sliver of natural lake is the third deepest in North America. But what's a mere fifteen hundred vertical feet of water? Coveting even more for their hungry electrical turbines, the Powers that Be (electrical variety) long ago built a damn (sic) that raised the water level a whole twenty-one more feet and turned a natural gem into just another reservoir with shoreline development to match. Traffic is heavy all the way.

By the time we pull into the East Bank trailhead at Ruby Creek, it's midafternoon. As we're cramming our packs for the easy stroll to our first night's camp, it starts raining. I'm ready before Branson, who has to carefully wrap his high-dollar camera gear against the wet. Anxious to get moving, I treat myself to a packless stroll up the jungly trail and immediately encounter bushes dripping with ripe wild raspberries. My favorites, huckleberries, will come later in the season. For now, these black-red gems will do just fine.

While I'm staining my gray beard red with the juicy fruits, along comes a family of down-trail hikers. Dressed in shorts, t-shirts, cheap plastic rain ponchos and goose flesh, the woman and teen-aged boy say hello but keep on truckin', anxious for the dry warmth of their waiting vehicle. The man, however, stops and engages me in conversation, from which I learn—the horror!—that Ross "Lake," which Branson and I have yet even to lay eyes on, is no lake at all but a friggin' *reservoir*. And predictably, its twelve thousand watery acres have been drawn down, down, down for power generation, creating what my dripping informant describes as "a filthy bathtub ring" around its entire shoreline (twenty-four miles long by two at the widest).

My shutterbug pal will love that, being already crippled by rain, clouds, fog, snow.

And there's more: This fleeing family prematurely abandoned the selfsame camp Branson and I are headed for tonight, not because of the rain or unsightly ring around the reservoir, but because they were run off by a pesky black bear that ignored their yelling, banging pots and throwing rocks. "Makes it kinda hard to sleep," says the man, a little embarrassed.

The bear doesn't bother me so much, since I'm packing pepper spray and will, if I must, administer a dose of aversive conditioning to the perilously emboldened beast (might save his fuzzy butt). What does bother me is—we didn't drive all the long way here to spend a week staring at no stinkin' reservoir ring.

Thus and so, I slog back to the trailhead and give Branson the news that I've been ill advised by the authorities. (Why accept the blame myself? Nobody else does these irresponsible days.) With just half a handful of daylight hours left, we need to *do something*, fast.

We do a quick map check, then reinsert ourselves into my wreckmobile and backtrack along the North Cascades Highway to Rainy Pass, where we pull in at the Lake Ann trailhead, elevation 4860 feet. Lake Ann lies at 5475 feet and only two miles distant. From there we figure, on the morrow, we can keep going, up and over Heather and Maple passes—6100 and 6600 feet respectively—for a two- or even three-day loop hike. If the snow will let us.

(It's not that I find snow so hateful, but just that I'm buried in the stuff for five months every winter and, hell, this is *July*; if we wanted snow-hiking, we'd have stayed in Colorado.)

As we buckle into our loads, the rain fizzles to a drizzle, stops, and a scarlet evening sky glows through. Good omens.

Upward.

It's serious forest here, the mud-soup trail shaded by a shaggy canopy of immense old-growth conifers (Doug-fir, lodgepole and ponderosa pine, Engelmann spruce and larch). We encounter patchy snow within minutes but continue on, at one point kicking tenuous toe-holds across a broad, steep, alga-pinked snow field of some modest danger. At a fork in the trail we find all but the top of the Lake Ann sign buried in white, and we're no longer hiking so much as post-holing. We poke around a little, but can find no level dry spot large enough to pitch a tent, much less see any hint of any lake.

With evening upon us and the day's warmth failing, things are beginning to get semi-serious. The rain resumes as we scurry back down-trail, striding past piping pikas and whistling marmots, blasting back across the icy avalanche chute, arriving at the trail-head just at dusk. Standing cold, sodden and frustrated in the rain and dark, we make a decision—illicit but practical—to bivouac here for the night. Hardly the deep-wilderness challenge we've come for, but adventure (which is rarely fun while it's happening) nonetheless.

ᗝ

Our wake-up call is an adolescent raven just getting its voice. At dawn's first crack he, or she, lodges in a tree above our humble nylon abode and commences squawking like Ross Parrot. During rare brief pauses, I hear the low rumble of a distant creek.

"Cascades"—a good and proper name for this place where the ubiquitous streams don't run or trickle or burble or flow or slip or slide along nearly so often as they come booming down through narrow, precipitous, log-and-boulder-choked chutes in foaming, *cascading* whitewater torrents. The mountains make them do it.

These are young mountains (as mountains go), brought into jagged existence within the past few-score million years via continental drift, tectonic buckling and volcanic up-chuck, glaciation and stream erosion (the old story). Still stark and sharp, the North Cascades embody some of the most convoluted geology in North America.

The average peak elevation here is only about seven grand, but the Puget Sound Trough lies just thirty miles from the Cascades' western flank—while most of my home state's famous fourteeners, I reflect, *begin* at around seven thousand feet, ciphering out to roughly equal vertical relief and grandeur.

Nor is it all ice and rock. Within this vast granitic jumble thrive more than fifteen hundred species of plants and two hundred of birds. One of which I could well do without just now.

We leave the raven ranting to him- or herself and motor east over Washington Pass. At 5477 feet, this is the highest point on the North Cascades Highway (Washington 20), the only roadway with gumption enough to cross the North Cascades east to west, and open only in summer at that. Even so, the view is more up than down: Sawing at the sky two thousand feet and more above us are Liberty Bell Mountain, the Minutmen, Early Winters Spires, Kangaroo and Snagtooth ridges and dozens more. It's a world of white up there, a world of wonder.

At the Early Winters Forest Service information center we stop for a belated bit of "pretrip" planning. On the advice of a nice young man, a Johnny Depp lookalike with one dangly earring, we decide to give a place called Hart's Pass a go. Its long, gravel access road (built for miners and mules in 1900, originally just thirty-six inches wide but a little wider now) is reported to be snow-free to almost timberline. Were we able to drive farther, says Ranger Depp, we'd be on the Slate Peak road, the highest roadway in Washington. Below the pass, we're assured, the landscape is a scenic quiltwork of "mostly" snow-free krummholz and subalpine meadows with abundant hiking opportunities, few hikers and no reservations required.

Off again, slouching back out into the wild wet yonder, following the Hart's Pass road west along the Methow River past the invisible ghost-town site of a mining camp called Robinson and north along Rattlesnake Creek, up and up through a painter's palette of summer mountain flora, including Indian paintbrush in vibrant red, white-flowered cow parsnips, purple asters, red and yellow shooting stars, pastel flax, blue-bonneted lupine and a lovely plethora of others mostly strange to our Rockies-trained eyes.

At midday we approach a barricade of snow marking the road's ad hoc terminus, just beyond a trailhead leading to the Pacific Crest thruway: "Windy Pass 4, Woody Pass 19, Canadian border 31" says the big wooden sign. This is Sunday, and the place is bustling with day hikers anxious to challenge the lingering snow and bitter alpine wind for the dubious boast of setting brief foot on the high-profile PCT.

Ignoring them, we saddle up and trudge off along an unsigned, obviously unmaintained trail meandering gently upward through a huge marshy meadow like God's own golf course toward a taiga of subalpine fir and, above that, gnarly krummholz and tundra. Mountain goat heaven up there, though the only white in sight just now is snow.

A mile or so along, amidst all this pristine splendor, some SOB has tossed a shiny new Coors can. With friends like this, nature doesn't need its many enemies. I stomp the filthy *basura* flat (pretending it's the litterer's skull) and stuff it in a sidepocket of my already overstuffed pack.

In time we abandon the pseudo-trail and wander untethered until early evening, when we happen into a small charismatic meadow set about by subalpine fir and alive with avalanche lilies, geraniums and many another, plus your basic spectacular if humble alpine array of moss and moss campion, lichen, dwarf juniper and silent sedimen-

tary rock. No jet contrails scar the (momentarily) cloudless sky and a
billion-buck vista reaches far into the southwest, beyond the earth's
curve, toward the brooding Pacific. The only sounds are the sluggish
buzzing of a few fat flies, the trickle of a snowmelt rill, the cheery twittering of anonymous birds. A tranquil contentment invests the whole.

I drop my pack and wander about, feeling light as alpine air,
mindful of the caution sign posted back at the trailhead: "Choose
another camping area if you see bears, dead animals or bear sign
such as tracks, droppings or diggings. Be alert!"

Although a scattering of grizzlies and numerous black bears
haunt these heights, I find no spoor of either, but only the dainty
tracks of mule deer. Too bad. A known lurking predatory presence
puts the wild back in wilderness and demands of visitors an ani-
mal-alertness and humbling respect for nature otherwise too often
forgotten.

❧

Persecution of the grizzly here, as throughout western North
America, began the moment white men first encountered the great
shaggy beasts. From 1827 to 1859 alone, the hides of 3788 grizzlies
were "harvested" hereabouts, as recorded in the blood-stained
records of the Hudson's Bay Company.

Today, across the entire ten thousand square-mile portion of the
North Cascades lying south of the Canadian border, there could be
fewer than a dozen grizzlies remaining. Maybe more. Nobody
knows for sure. Happily, this place is designated in the U.S. Fish and
Wildlife Service's Grizzly Bear Recovery Plan as one of six official
"grizzly recovery zones." Sadly, a lack of funding on the federal level
(exacerbated by the current anti-nature Congress), together with a
sluggish Washington state wildlife bureaucracy and negative pressure from logging and other special interests, have effectively stifled

Cascades grizzly recovery—which is to say, reintroduction. At least for the nonce.

Yet the great bears are about, albeit ghostly and few, and that knowledge enriches my pleasure immeasurably. It is, in point of fact, a primary reason Branson and I decided to drive two thousand miles for a week's helter-skelter hiking when we have plenty of perfectly good mountains at home. Without its remnant populations of grizzlies and wolves, the North Cascades would be just another visually spectacular "wilderness" with its heart chopped out.

∾

With our modest camp set, Branson wanders off for his traditional sunset solo (God only knows what he does out there, alone, but he's done it every night we've ever camped together for years). I grab topographic map and compass and walk to a nearby cliff and plop down to try and put names to a few of the peaks framing this big blue-green world.

That looming dark beauty backlighted by the lowering sun is of course the Golden Horn, floating 8806 feet in the sky and named for the dominant geologic formation hereabouts, the Golden Horn Batholith, a granitic mass dating to the early Tertiary (somewhat before my time). In the south rise the aptly named Needles, together with the jagged line of Delancy Ridge and various other eye-popping etceteras.

Living glaciers abound—some 600 throughout the North Cascades withal, 318 in the park alone—patiently sculpting an anachronistic Pleistocene landscape of aretes, cirques, horns, moraines, troughs, U-shaped and hanging valleys, tarns—the whole lovely lot—most all of it carved within the past two dozen millennia. That's Robinson Mountain behind us there, meaning we're just within the bounds of the Pasayten Wilderness. Maybe. Not that it matters.

What does matter is being in a pristine place *alone.* It's Touron prime-time, and the highway miles below carries a steady effluvium of traffic day and night, mostly Washington locals. Yet we've seen only a scattering of cars at even the most popular and accessible trailheads, the most of them awaiting the return of day hikers. This stands in sharp contrast to my backyard wilderness, the Weminuche, where most summer trailheads are perennially jammed with cars and horse trailers and the "wilderness" is quite literally hopping.

Which is not to say the North Cascades have no overcrowding problems. In some popular day-use areas accessed from the Pacific side, alpine flora has been so trampled that management agencies have resorted to raising native plants in greenhouses and transplanting them to the damaged tundra.

But not here. Not yet.

The sky begins to darken and I mosey back campward, stepping over the miniature haystack remains of some hardy little rodent's winter home. The lupines up here have yet to flower and may not this brief wintry summer. In a brilliant explosion of crimson and gold, a male western tanager flashes by.

We could, I suppose, backpack for days through this verdant webwork of subalpine forest, meadow and cliff, dodging along below the snow line. But why? Once you've carried a pack far enough to be free from the detritus of what Abbey aptly dubbed syphilisation, one spectacular wilderness base camp is just about as good as another.

Or so say I. I who no longer rate the worth of a hike by miles hiked. A backpack is merely a tool to get you into the wilds with what you need to enjoy being there, here. It is not, should not be allowed to become, a taskmaster. Let others hump the hard miles. I've been there, plenty of times, and it can be good. But these days, having attained the hard-won rank of semi-old fart, I prefer to experience wild lovely places slowly, intimately, rather than coming and going in a sweaty blur.

Shucks, I hardly ever hump more than eight or ten miles a day any more. At least not in the mountains.

A male blue grouse, big as a bantam rooster, struts boldly into my path and mounts a downed log in full bombast: tail fanned like a diminutive tom turkey, neck flowers bloomed in red and white, red-and-gold-barred head a'bobbing—a classic courtship display, albeit more than two months late per the norm down in my southern Rockies stamping grounds. Like bachelor Branson, just another wild and crazy guy.

The air grows suddenly chill and dew falls early, almost like rain. Branson returns just at dark and I kindle my trusty alcohol stove—slow as Grandpa on a January morning, but cheap, lightweight, compact and virtually idiot-proof (a real plus in my case)—and put on a feast of dehydrated soup and noodles simmered in unfiltered snowmelt, saltines and sharp cheddar on the side.

Another sunset promise written in scarlet. Another belying downpour in the night.

∞

Morning mountains wreathed in cloud. Strong slow coffee and two granola bars for breakfast. On such a drippy, dreary day it's easy to convince easygoing Branson to leave the tent up and our packs inside while we day hike haphazardly roundabouts—I'll not subject you to all the exhilarating details.

Upon our return at sunset, we're met by a lone raven circling slow and low … welcoming us back to camp? More likely just curious. And no doubt hungry. Like us.

After dinner, as always in bear country, I walk an honest hundred yards downwind of camp with food and trash stashed in waterproof stuff sacks, and hang 'em high from a protruding limb, safe from nocturnal prowlers. No big deal.

∾

Morning again, this one sunny. So far. As we're headed down, out and on to other adventures of discovery, a piglet-sized black bear cub waddles across just ahead, spots us and quicker than a sneaked wink at a highschool reunion is ten feet up the nearest tree. From the perceived safety of this vantage he, or maybe she, peeks at us like an overgrown squirrel. We keep moving, not wishing to meet momma bear, glancing back over our shoulders. Soon the cub shinnies back to earth and disappears into the forest.

With plenty of daylight still on our hands (and faces) after trucking back down to the blacktop, we decide to squander a leisurely hour or so on a hike to a classic glacial tarn called Rainy Lake. The one-mile trail climbs a very moderate grade, is blacktopped all the way and ends in a railed overlook platform just above the pellucid (and apparently fishless) water. This is the most sublime close-up scene we've yet stumbled into during our somewhat schizophrenic exploration of these northernmost Cascades, and the public money spent to make it accessible to wheelchair hikers is money well spent indeed.

Oh well, time again to start thinking about a room with a view for the night, preferably with possibilities for an extended hike on the morrow. After another quick map check we head for a place called Cedar Falls. The Cedar Creek trail, though uphill and muddy—it's raining for a change—offers a pleasant stroll amongst ponderosa giants. Cedar Falls, as it turns out, is in fact plural—a double tumble of some sixty feet. The upper fall is most impressive of the two, its torrent leaping straight out before giving in to gravity's pull. Forming the lip of the fall is a protruding slab of wet-black rock. More of the same, smaller, shelve out here and there down the way, providing homes to hanging gardens of ferns and other waterworld plants. In one shelf pool halfway down, a dapper dipper dips for dinner.

The rain stops, the overcast parts, the sun appears and rainbowed vapor clouds drift like torpid ghosts from peak to peak above us. Five glorious minutes of this meteorological Nirvana, and the gloom and rain return. Even so, Branson and I allow as how this might be a nice place to crash for the night, the roar, wind and spray of the falls notwithstanding.

We make our way out along the cliff to a narrow ledge overlooking the cold blue pool of the lower fall, in whose torrent tumbles— by George, it's a big blue tent. Collapsed of course, most likely blown off this open blustery ledge.

Across the narrow gorge of the thundering creek rises a near-vertical slope verdant with spruce, fir—and back in there somewhere I suppose, given the name of the place, cedar—plus ferns, mosses and countless unknown so-ons. Anybody temerarious enough to try bushwhacking through this montane jungle would need a machete and a miracle to come out alive: the dense forest canopy would stifle any Global Positioning System, a map and compass would be next to useless with no visible horizon in any direction, and the ferocious snarl of vine maple, alder, stinging nettle, devil's club and more would rip the shirt off your back then have a go at the tender wet flesh beneath.

Taking a hint from the forlorn tent tossing in the tumult below, we reconsider bivouacking here. But if not here, where? The old question. I break out my limp "waterproof" map and peruse the mind-boggling possibilities.

This is hardly shaping up as the deep-wilderness adventure I'd envisioned at the outset. But then, reality happens, even in the outdoors. Who knows what wonders may emerge in retrospect?

Besides, we ain't quite done yet.

As we move out, uptrail, the sky clears and a hot-pink sunset warms the evening. Here we go again.

19

A Wild and Fierce Freedom

WE ARE HUFFING UP Glacier National Park's ungodly steep Loop Trail, a friend and I, bulging packs chafing our sweaty backs. Having launched this little adventure from a scenic pull-out along the park's eye-popping Going-to-the-Sun Road, we are headed for a place called Granite Park. Up where the grizzer bears roam.

Back home in Colorado, we have so few grizzlies left, they seem more like ghosts than bears. So I've come here to Glacier, on the northern border of Montana and these United States of America, in hopes of observing a few of these beautiful monsters where they still exist in relatively healthy, albeit dwindling numbers. To facilitate and enliven the quest, I've enlisted as my guide former park bear manager Neal Wedum, who animates our hike with item after item from his bottomless bag of "Gee whiz!" bear-scare stories.

Like the time he was patrolling a remote park trail and heard a crunching sound somewhere above him. "I looked up," he says, "into the eyes of the biggest bear I've ever seen. The boar grizzly was lying behind a clump of brush on a little bench maybe fifty feet above the trail, its head raised and looking right at me. A big chunk of bloody meat sagged from his jaws and saliva drooled from his muzzle. The adrenaline rush almost knocked me off my feet. My first thought was that the bear was eating a hiker, and having surprised him on his meal, I'd be dessert."

Wedum kept walking, even as he slipped the safety off his canister of pepper spray. Not stopping or running was apparently the right move, because the behemoth bear merely watched intently until the interloper had passed on down the trail and out of sight.

When safely beyond the threat, Wedum did what only a seasoned backcountry ranger and grizzly expert should attempt, and climbed through a finger of subalpine firs leading up the cliff to a narrow shelf, then worked cautiously across until he was directly above the feeding bear. "I had to know," he says, attempting to explain away such flagrant temerity, "what was being eaten. Or who."

The carnivore's feast turned out to be a full-curl bighorn ram. "The sheep probably died in a fall and the grizzly's nose led him to it. Bears can't catch healthy bighorns, but they can smell a dead one from miles away."

After radioing instructions that the trail be closed a safe distance either side of the danger, Wedum eased back down the slope, keeping to the trees, then inched forward until he was watching the feasting boar from what, in retrospect, was "too damn close." Just as Neal was becoming almost relaxed in the presence of this six hundred (or more) pounds of teeth, claws and temper, and with no warning whatsoever, the bear exploded down the hill directly toward him, ending its bluff charge just twenty feet from one badly shaken park ranger.

"That," Wedum recalls, "pretty much got my attention."

The canister of pepper spray had long since been returned to its holster, the safety clip replaced. "No matter," my hiking companion tells me now. "I wouldn't have had time to spray that bear even if I'd had the canister in my hand; he came that fast."

The panting grizzly glared at the interloper for "a real long time," then turned and shuffled back up the slope toward its meat cache … only to whirl and charge again, this time getting bad-breath close before abruptly stopping.

"He was so near I could *feel* his breath as well as smell it. The look on his face was clearly saying, 'OK pal, I've warned you twice. Now move along or you're lunch meat.' I moved along."

And so do we, ever up.

A little farther on, Wedum points to scuff marks on a slender birch. "Right here," says my cheerful guide, "is where a down-trail hiker ran into a grizzly sow with two cubs. The man started up this little tree, his boots scuffing the bark as he clamped his feet to the trunk and attempted to climb. He didn't quite make it. That old sow grabbed him by a leg, bit deep into his calf, yanked him down and slapped him around just enough to get her message across: 'Don't mess with my cubs.' He was lucky; able to walk out."

Yes, *such* luck.

ॐ

Most every summer for God only recalls how many years now, I've wheedled the time and money for a Glacier camping vacation. Because the Northern Continental Divide Ecosystem, of which Glacier is the beating heart, still shelters representative samples of all of its most magnificent native megafauna—grizzlies, wolves, wolverines, moose, wapiti, bighorns, mountain goats, ospreys, eagles, loons—by my lights, it's the most magic-filled place in the lower forty-eight.

Here Caroline and I come to hike, camp, fish, canoe, graze on bush-ripened berries, make love amongst the ferns and mosquitoes and lie awake in wonder at the haunting calls of loons and, yes, wolves. And we frequently manage to scare ourselves sleepless conjuring up toothy monsters *out there* in the vast blackness just beyond the gossamer walls of our tent. Thus is generated the spiritual voltage that electrifies the Glacier backcountry experience.

This time, I've come to crank that voltage to the max, and a finer grizzly guide than Neal Wedum I'd be strapped to find: native Montanan, Glacier backcountry ranger for eighteen years, bear management team leader for six.

At five-foot-nine, 155 pounds and half a century, Neal Wedum remains the unlikely champion "human mule" of Glacier Park, having backpacked loads as heavy as 120 pounds into these precipitous old mountains—wearing sport sandals, no less. Once, he and a fellow ranger bet a case of beer with a wrangler that working in relays, they could backpack a seventy-pound, four-foot-long steel propane tank (full) up the Loop Trail four miles to Granite Park faster than a mule. They won. Even now, Neal's oversized backpack is bulging with such wilderness "necessities" as a 703-page hardbound copy of *Mahatma Gandhi*. Heavy reading.

∞

While breaking for lunch on a ledge with a million-dollar view (they're a dime a dozen here), we're passed by a couple of unburdened day hikers whose approach is announced by the annoying tinkle of cheap copper "bear bells."

Local wisdom: How do you tell the difference between grizzly and black bear scats? The grizzly flops are the big ones with bells in them.

Jangling through the boonies like some amplified Tinkerbell is anathema to my notion of a quality wilderness experience. Yet I understand the park's motivation for encouraging backcountry hikers to engage in singing, whooping, loud talking and Tinkerbelling: a surprise run-in with a grizzly could spell disaster for all involved. When Neal and I hike Glacier together (this isn't the first time), we talk as the mood strikes us, maybe a little louder than necessary sometimes, but staunchly eschew the hackneyed shouts of "Hey, bear!" that so frequently disturb the otherwise sublime tranquillity of this Pleistocene wonderland, trusting our safety instead to Neal's highly cultivated "nose" for pending grizzly danger.

"After a while," he'll tell you, "you get to where you can sense a grizzly presence, like some people can sense an approaching storm or an earthquake." Must be true: my old pal Peacock feels it too, as do an experienced handful of others.

As we pass through a small clearing resplendent with glacier lilies, giant cow parsnips, big lacy beargrass plumes and Indian paintbrush red as lust, Neal says casually, "We call this place Mauling Meadow."

I daren't ask why.

A little farther along, we come to the spot where a recent and perplexing grizzly disaster was acted out—the mauling death of John Petranyi, aged forty, killed and fed upon by a grizzly sow and her two subadult cubs.

On the morning of October 3, 1992, Petranyi was hiking alone down this selfsame Loop Trail after spending the night at the Granite Park backcountry campground. He apparently surprised the bears at close range on or near the trail. The sow did what grizzly mothers are programmed by natural selection to do in such instances, and launched a preemptive assault on this sudden threat to her cubs.

Evidence suggests the sow broke off her attack and retreated after giving Petranyi only a light mauling; fairly common. Perhaps, had he played dead until the bears were good and gone, he might have saved himself. But Petranyi apparently attempted to flee—perhaps calling for help as he ran—thus exciting the bears' prey-pursuit instincts and provoking a second attack. This time, the grizzlies dragged Petranyi to a nearby wooded promontory and ...

A few days later, following multi-agency consultations, the offending bear family were hunted down and killed.

It's hard to keep such horrifying incidents from creeping into your dreams when camping in Glacier, especially in the backcountry. Yet, when you consider the intensity of the overlapping populations of humans (about two million visitors annually) and grizzlies (at least two hundred) here, and when you crank in the unforgivable rudeness and blatant *stupidity* of many park visitors—stashing food and smelly trash in their tents, hiking alone after dark, intentionally approaching and harassing bears and in countless other ways trolling for trouble—all such things considered, it's a wonder, a gift in fact, that Glacier's grizzlies show the remarkable tolerance they do.

Which is to say: Since its creation in 1910, the park has known just nine deaths by grizzly, with six of the nine being attributed to human-habituated "garbage bears," a threat park officials go to great lengths these days to minimize by trucking out trash and enforcing strict backcountry food-handling regulations. "A fed bear is a dead bear," we often hear. A fed bear could also be a dead human, but that doesn't rhyme.

Maulings and other physical encounters with bears are less uncommon, yet still average only two per summer; your odds of being chomped by a Glacier grizzly are roughly one in a million.

To put all of this in perspective: in a lifetime of hiking the park's backcountry, on trail and off, including many intentional, line-of-duty encounters with known "problem" bears, Neal Wedum has been bluff-charged six times, treed twice and never even scratched by a grizzly. (So far.) Across those same years, he's helped rescue several people seriously injured by falls and other park mishaps far more common but far less glamorous or newsworthy than bear attacks.

∾

We're nearing Granite Park campground now, finally, and my mentor feels moved to assure me of its safety.

"I've spent entire nights sitting on a hill above here, looking down on this ridge with a military starlight scope. Grizzlies come and go along the natural travel corridors on either side all night long, only a few dozen yards below campers and tents, ignoring them completely. So long as folks obey the rules, it's as safe a camp as you can have in intense grizzly country."

Most reassuring.

The original Granite Park campground—a tiny meadow bisected by the Loop Trail and now restored to the grizzly travel corridor and feeding site nature intended it to be—was a different story. It was there, just after midnight on the bad night of August 13, 1967, that park employee Julie Hegelson was dragged from her sleeping bag and fatally mauled by a grizzly. Julie's male companion was also attacked, but survived. The sow identified as the culprit had been hanging around Granite Park for years, attracted by garbage and handouts.

Didn't park officials know they'd located the campground on a natural bear runway? "No," says Neal. "They didn't worry about such things back then. There had never been a grizzly-caused death in the fifty-seven-year history of the park, and they assumed the bears were benign."

Incredibly, that same night in 1967, at a popular backcountry camp called Trout Lake, another young camper, Michele Koons, was killed by another "garbage bear." This tragic coincidence supplied the meat for Jack Olsen's adrenalizing *Night of the Grizzlies*—a book you may not want to read just before visiting a place like Glacier or Yellowstone.

The new Granite Park campground, where we're now resting, consists of four tent sites staggered along a narrow timbered ridge with spectacular views in every direction, an open-air privy, a food preparation area and two high, hook-topped poles from which to suspend food bags. No campfires allowed.

"The only animal problems we've had here," says Neal, "are deer brushing against tents at night. Scares hell out of folks."

I can't imagine why.

When my quadriceps have quit burning from the hike in, we head up the mountain to visit the medieval-looking Granite Park Chalet—a wilderness oxymoron written in native stone. This stately old building was built in 1914 and for decades offered modest but sturdy backcountry shelter and home-cooked meals to hikers. In 1987, the Chalet was designated a National Historic Landmark—only to be closed recently due to water, sewage, maintenance and political problems. The structure is being renovated even now and the park intends to reopen it as soon as possible.

Which will be none too soon for Neal Wedum, who voices a popular local sentiment when he remarks that "the Chalet is as much a part of the Glacier tradition as the bears and the mountains. And the huckleberry pies they baked here were the best in the world. I had a deal with the baker: I'd bring her fresh huckleberries in exchange for free pie. Once, a friend and I found a couple of huge fresh grizzly scats loaded with perfect berries—bears have really inefficient guts, and what doesn't get chewed usually doesn't get digested. Feeling ornery, we picked out all the whole berries, washed them in a creek and took them back to the Chalet. The baker made two pies, which the staff ate and raved about."

Did the baker know the history of those berries?

"I may have forgotten to mention it."

Did Neal have a slice of this delicious huckleberry griz-scat pie?

"No way!"

Whether you're for or against the Chalet's presence here, the cloud-piercing promontory upon which it sits offers one of the most sublime mountain vistas in the known universe, as well as lucrative grizzly watching. That's why I've lugged along a spotting scope, which I now train down upon a sprawling subalpine vale south of Granite Park—a mile-square bowlful of grizzly paradise appropriately named Bear Valley.

In three hours of hard glassing I see nary a single hair of bear. What I do see is enough faulted, folded, upthrust and tilted, glaciated and splendorous ancient sea-bed scenery to fuel a lifetime of burning nostalgia, all backdropped by the distant slender veil of Bird Woman

Falls. Between she and me, a lone golden eagle, aloof and insouciant, hangs without effort on some invisible thermal. How I envy her.

Losing hope, I make one last perusal of the valley before breaking for dinner and—hot damn!—spot a huge dark animal loafing across a big gray slab of granite.

I whoop and Neal joins me, and for the next several minutes we watch the bear as it feeds among the quiltwork of tiny meadows, turns over rocks and rips apart fallen logs looking for insects, digs for roots, melts into then reappears from dense copses of subalpine spruce and fir and otherwise indulges and enjoys its wild and fierce freedom. The animal is a dark glossy brown with massive muscles that ripple visibly with every step. The late afternoon sun glints on tiny eyes as hard and impenetrable as obsidian.

Here, I reflect, is the flesh-and-fur incarnation of the wildness in which Thoreau advised resides the preservation of the world. The preservation of *my* world, at least.

Suddenly, the big grizzly breaks from feeding, looks back over its left shoulder, then sprints away at racehorse speed, disappearing into the trees. We spend the next hour in a fruitless search for whatever it was that had frightened a bear so huge you'd think it would run from nothing smaller than a T-Rex. Just another of nature's invigorating mysteries.

∾

The night is cold and happily uneventful. I rise at dawn and retire to the Chalet to resume my magnified search for grizzlies. Neal soon joins me and we decide to invest the midmorning in hiking the Highline Trail—a major backcountry byway tracing along just below the Continental Divide—glassing pockets of habitat Wedum knows to be frequented by bears.

"What grizzlies like, what they *need*," my friend explains as we walk, calling on his master's education in biology and lifetime of field experience, "is room to move, clean water, dense woods to shelter in and plenty of high-calorie, easily digestible food."

In Glacier country, the most important bear foods are huckleberries in the fall and glacier lilies (better known as avalanche lilies in the Southern Rockies) spring through summer.

Glacier lilies: grizzlies dig these yellow mountain lovelies by the hundreds for their marble-sized, white-meated, starch-rich root bulbs. Attentive hikers appreciate the little pixies for their cheerful beauty and the sublime surroundings in which they erupt by the thousands—subalpine meadows and alpine tundra.

After an hour or so of speed walking—I can maintain Neal's killer pace for a while, but not forever—we spot a series of bear digs starting just below the trail. We drop down to investigate, finding the open slope pocked with scores of grizzly excavations. Neal explains that shovel-sized clumps of sod flipped over in digs a few inches deep and up to a hundred square feet in area are the spoor of grizzlies grubbing for roots. More impressive but less common are waist-deep pits with rocks big as basketballs tossed out, where a meat-hungry bear has back-hoed after a ground squirrel or marmot.

Obviously, bear digs are important sign to recognize, and to avoid, when selecting a campsite in grizzly country.

Onward, to a place called Ahern Pass, where a lingering snow slide blocks further progress. Just beyond, Neal points out the shelf where, three years before, he met his ram-eating boar.

Good place for a break.

We're sitting and talking and glassing for wildlife when a lone young hiker comes striding up the trail behind us, says "Howdy," sits down and hauls from his outsized pack climbing boots, crampons and ice ax. My conviction that, with so much youthful confidence and fine equipment, he'll breeze painlessly across the slide is given the lie within his first few steps, when the young man slips, goes rocketing down the ice and out across several feet of exposed scree shards before managing a last-second ax-arrest a foot short of plunging over the cliff's edge to certain, absolute, immutable death. Undaunted, the young man stands—his right hand and leg are smeared with blood—grins, shrugs and continues on, somewhat more carefully now. We hold our collective breath until he makes it safely across.

This incident prompts Neal to comment that when people think of danger in Glacier, they invariably think of grizzlies. Yet bears rank way down the line as killers here, trailing drownings (forty-eight), heart attacks (twenty-seven), car crashes (twenty-five), falls while hiking (twenty-one) and climbing accidents (eighteen), for a total of nine grizzly deaths alongside 138 from other causes since 1913.

"I have friends," says Neal, "who've hiked and camped in Glacier for thirty years and have never even seen a grizzly."

Only, I think, because they weren't really looking.

∾

It's midafternoon by the time we return to our Granite Park digs, where we dally just long enough to raid our food bags for snacks before scrambling down to a secluded promontory on a rocky lip directly above Bear Valley. Any grizzlies seen from here, I reckon, will be plenty close enough.

And the *view*—the aptly named Heaven's Peak dominates the west, the jagged rampart of the Garden Wall saws at the sky along the eastern horizon, Logan Pass (the highest paved point on any park road) lies low in the south, with Oberlin, Reynolds, Clements, Cannon and other rocky spires jutting up in wild and glorious disarray all around. Purple mountains' majesty, you bet.

We glass intently, but soon grow woozy under the warm July sun; only the incessant pestering of mosquitoes and carnivorous deer flies keeps us awake.

"Once," says my droopy-eyed companion, "on a day just like today, I came down here, right here, and fell asleep. A couple of hours later

I was awakened by splashing noises from that little pond over there." Neal gestures to a tiny pool no more than fifty yards away, shallow and lucent and surrounded by an earthly heaven of beargrass, purple gentian, shooting stars, mountain bluebells and dandelions. "When I opened my eyes, I was looking at a sow and two cubs playing in the water. Didn't have any trouble staying awake after that."

A big black-and-gray Clark's nutcracker swoops in and perches atop a perfect little Christmas tree just below us, scolding, it seems, our very existence. Moments later, the resident eagle appears at the far edge of the valley, as if summoned by the Clark's ill-tempered scolds: a six-foot feathered exclamation point on a flawless sky.

After two hours of sun, scenery and bugs, but no bears, we groan to our feet and chug up-mountain to the backcountry ranger quarters, located adjacent to the Chalet and currently occupied by a burly, red-headed ex-Marine named Kim Peach, a mate of Neal's from the bear management team.

And wouldn't you know it, even as we arrive, Ranger Peach spots a grizzly—directly below the promontory we abandoned only minutes ago.

For the next half hour we watch as this big, ruddy bruin with a muzzle the color of parchment and silvery guard hairs across its camel-humped shoulders browses, noses around and digs. At one point, having found a dense patch of glacier lilies, the bear settles back onto his ample haunches and uses both front paws—through my scope I can see the ivory claws clearly, as thick and long as a big man's fingers—to roll back a huge wad of turf, which he lifts to his muzzle and nibbles at ... like a squirrel with a pine cone or a fat man eating corn on the cob. We are all saddened when this entertaining beast eventually wanders into the trees and fails to reappear.

After a ho-hum dinner of boil-in-the-pouch turkey and dressing, Neal and I return to our vigil. Within ten minutes—I can't believe the luck—Neal has yet another bear under glass.

218

Out There

This one, like the previous two, is big and fat, weighing maybe four hundred pounds. But unlike the others, both of which were dark, this animal has hair the color of autumn grain, the classic grizzly pelage. I'm acutely aware that this lovely blond beast, if properly provoked, could rip my lungs out with a single swipe of clawsome paw. Yet I feel a baffling affection for and desire to get closer to "her." A potentially fatal attraction.

Before that foolish urge can be acted on, the fearsome beauty steps into the long evening shadows and dissolves into the foggy realm of memory.

Just before dark, four sweaty day-hikers straggle in, looking for a privy. When they seem in no hurry to leave, the residual park ranger in Neal suggests that they get the hell on down the trail as fast as possible without running, keeping close together and making *lots* of noise. They shrug, not apparently appreciating the sagacity of this advice, but soon move on. If they knew the history of the Loop Trail, I reflect, they'd sprout wings and fly down. They just might anyhow (as angels).

∾

Come morning, our third and last here at Granite Park, we hike back down to the sunny, soporific promontory of the splashing bears, hoping for one more glimpse of that gorgeous blond grizzly. But the local bruins are sleeping late—or, more likely, have bedded early—and visions of huckleberry milkshakes down at Apgar Village are growing ever more compelling (I'll make damn sure they don't get their berries from Wedum).

After a couple of uneventful hours, we climb back up to Granite Park, pack our packs and point our sunburnt noses reluctantly down the mountain. Even though he's spent hundreds of nights up here, Neal is overtly sad to leave, explaining "It gets in your blood."

Does it ever.

We make a fast hike down—past the disquieting Petranyi mauling site, through the erstwhile Night of the Grizzlies campground and the florid Mauling Meadow, past the boot-scuffed grizzly tree.

About a mile from trail's end, Neal, hiking ahead of me as always, stops suddenly and whispers, "Look here." I look, and there amidst the grasses, ferns and giant cow parsnips just off the trail is a hot-fresh grizzly dig. And another. And a third.

"Those weren't here when we came up the other day," says I.

Neal drops to his knees and examines the dark, damp soil, the torn vegetation. "No," he agrees. "These digs are no more than a few hours old, made last night or early this morning."

I have a good look around, fingering the canister of bear spray holstered on my belt, before stooping for a closer look. In the largest of the excavations I find a big twisted heap of bear scat, green-white with undigested roots of glacier lily, odorless and so shockingly fresh it's still warm and oozing moisture.

A quarter-mile farther along, we find a second series of recent digs; clearly, this bear was walking the trail. I think of those four cocky hikers last night and shiver. By the time they could have gotten this far, down deep in the belly of this forest prime-evil (sic), the night would have been black as death. And this bear must have already been in the immediate neighborhood, as it probably is still.

Had there been an "incident" here last night, to whom would media and public sentiment attach the blame—blatantly careless hikers, or a "killer grizzly"?

Neal Wedum is suffering similar thoughts. "If only people could learn to cut bears as much slack as bears cut us," he says, "grizzlies wouldn't be an endangered species."

I'm reminded of something Doug Peacock said not long ago, as we sat in his Sonoran Desert backyard and sipped Black Jack on ice while Gambel's quail and mourning doves peeped and cooed all around us. "If we can't be big enough to set aside a few last-ditch preserves for an animal as intelligent, magnificent and manlike as the grizzly," Doug mused, "we have little chance of long-term survival as a species; we'll destroy nature, then we'll destroy ourselves."

Peacock clearly is a pessimist. And you know what they say about pessimists: they're optimists in possession of the facts.

20

Moonshine

LATE AUGUST, late day, mid-life.

For the past half hour, a dozen Colorado pronghorns have been grazing carelessly in a grassy bowl a few hundred yards below me; courageously close by antelope standards. Just moments ago a score or so more appeared on the southern horizon, half a mile out, feeding fast as caribou toward the base of the long, narrow knoll where I'm sitting in plain sight, binoculars in one hand, a cup in the other, next-to-nothing on my mind and fatigue in my bones from a long day adrift in nature.

Life is one long process of getting tired, whined that old dog Sammy Butler—and damned if he wasn't right.

At only fifty, it's painful to admit that I'm already slowing down, growing ever less interested in exertion for exertion's sake, ever more content just to sit and watch and reflect. A young man fears that by going too slow he risks missing something. An older man knows that by going too fast he risks missing everything.

Until quite recently, I had to *move* to enjoy the great outdoors—to bag the next crest, probe the valley beyond, to see as much as possible, albeit in a sweaty blur. Seeing is still the ticket, but lately I'm learning to enjoy the view as much from my ass as from my feet. Maybe more. I'll get physical again come morning, made restless by a good night's rest. But for the nonce, armed with a cheap cigar and a flask of the penultimate Irish whiskey ("Every man should have his Dew!"), I'm content just to be here, *right here,* dead-center this big, empty, high-rolling plain on this balmy August evening, alone but hardly lonely, watching a good day die.

Watching. As churning clouds of orange and lavender, like lazy aurora borealis, curtain the setting sun with psychedelic bands of living color. And listening, as a lone coyote heralds the incipient moonrise and pronghorns sneeze in nervous reply. For all of this and a whole lot more, I am profoundly grateful. The key to contentment, I'm learning, is an attitude of gratitude.

Just recently, the well-loved writer, artist and naturalist Ann Zwinger—a thoughtful friend who shares my boundless passion for wild nature—told me of having toured a museum where her attention was captured by a hand-blown jar dating from third century Cologne. It was, she noted, beautifully etched with a hunting scene and the epigraph *Vita Bona Fruamur Felices*: "Let us fortunate ones enjoy the good life."

Amen Ann, and pass the Dew.

Life *is* good, or can be, should be, if far more fragile than most of us ever realize in time to make it work. I'm lucky that way. This past spring, strange things started happening to my body. The first doctor I visited told me it was probably nothing to worry about but that I "could" have a particularly nasty type of cancer. That "could" became "do" in my paranoid mind, and let me tell you, friends—it put me through some changes.

Most memorably, my life priorities—those blessings to be recalled on my deathbed with a smile and a tear—flashed through my head as big and bright as Las Vegas marquees: waking in the night close and warm beside my sweet Caroline ... laughter-filled evenings in the company of a few true friends ... and doing exactly what I'm doing now, *out here.*

(Interlude: A hummingbird moth big as a B-52 just splash-landed in my hooch! I shoo it away but it comes looping back for more. This time I let it be and it doesn't drink all that much before staggering happily off into the shimmering twilight. Bartender for bugs ... is that what I've come to? Which reminds me: A friend recently recounted having mentioned my name in conversation when some joker interjected, "Oh, I know him; he's that writer guy who likes to smoke and drink!" Well, yes, I suppose I do, especially at night near the glowing warmth of a campfire—drawn, you could say, like a moth. But always and only in moderation, that elusive key to a life of happy vice.)

Anyhow, so there I was, depressed and defeatist, compulsively composing and revising my own eulogy, brimming with self-disgust, reminding myself that *cowards die many times before their deaths* (Willy the Shake), and, closer to home, *the fear of death follows from the fear of life. A man who lives fully is prepared to die at any time.*

True enough, Ed. But neither can we deny the undeniable fact that, as old Tom Browne would say (in fact said), *the long habit of living indisposeth us for dying.* Or, as Woody Allen so succinctly lays it down, *it's not that I'm afraid to die. I just don't want to be there when it happens.*

Me too.

At any rate and eventually, after four more doctors and months spent slouching through a purgatory of physical pain and existential angst, things sorted themselves out to the extent that I can now say, like Mark Twain, that reports of my death were exaggerations. Too old to die young, too young to die old. Nor am I complaining.

The upshot of that life-altering scare is that now I strive not only to tell, but to *show* my wife how much I love her, as if every day were the last. The same with my little band of close friends, though cautiously with a couple, so as not to embarrass the macho bastards.

And I've by-god doubled my time outdoors. More hiking and camping. More fishing and hunting. More canoeing and carefree careening around the backyard of beyond. More honest *living* while the living's good.

And no time like the present.

∾

As the sun sinks and the pronghorns fade to ghostly shadows, I retreat to my modest camp among the trees. With wood still damp from an afternoon thunderstorm, I re-enact Man's ancient quest for fire. That happy challenge accomplished, I refill my cup (one part creek water, one part Tullamore Dew; no ice tonight) and scoot up close to the companionable flames.

What a strange and wonderful place is this. Not your typical horizonless sagebrush antelope flat, but scenic basin and range country: rugged, rolling, cliff-framed, heavily vulcanized, tree-studded, sheltering numerous verdant side-pockets grown withers deep in yellow-flowering rabbitbrush. Average elevation, 8400 feet. Federal land: sublime by nature but brutally overgrazed each spring by a blight of domestic sheep. (Running short of traditional markets, now they're putting "lamb" in dog food! And look at the price we and the American wilds are paying for it!)

What else? A few stunted prickly pear. An occasional hornet's nest of yucca. Pygmy pines most everywhere (but curiously, not a one of their symbiotic sisters, genus *Juniperus*).

In the end—overlooking as best you can the mess "wise use" has made—this is one of the most hauntingly beautiful places on earth. A virtual window into our Pleistocene past, as if the antediluvian mists had only this morning lifted.

Back then, around the close of the latest (hardly the last) ice age, folks earned their livings hereabouts by ambushing mammoth and (when those ran out) wide-horned bison that came to drink from ice-gouged potholes filled with glacial meltwater. The pronghorn was here then too; had been for twenty million years. A true survivor, your wily prongy—unlike mammoth, giant bison and the gloriously barbaric lifestyles of their two-legged predators. Sigh ...

You've heard the lament, "I was born a hundred years too late." For me, it's ten millennia. At the very least.

ᔛ

All too soon, black dark cometh and the birdth doth falleth mute. Heat lightning, its growl tamed to a purr by distance, flashes in the eastern sky.

Time passes. The fire is burning low and so am I when the moon finally appears, a revelation in gold, climbing free of a cloud-wall black as fear.

Lunatic that I am, I fumble for my binoculars—big Commie military jobs, the Mercedes of low-light optics, Cold War surplus that once helped East German border guards spot their happy countrymen as they attempted to climb to freedom.

(A wall to keep people *in?* Hardly our problem here in America. *Vita bona fruamur felices!*)

I point my mighty optics moonward ... but can't bear the sight for long; the brilliance and mystery are all too much.

Somewhere in the invisible distance, a great-horned owl queries the night. *Such* a night! What was it you sang, brother Marley ... *There's a natural mystic flowing through the air.*

Or maybe just through my brain cells.

Another slash of Dew and my eyes dew too. Moonstruck (as it were), happy to be alive, I am reduced yet again to paltry poesy.

MOONSHINE
What I like most
about good whiskey
drunk
on moonlit campfire nights
is this ...
it lets me weep
unselfconsciously
in the presence
of truth and beauty.

But enough!

Back to "reality." I drain the dregs of my drink, struggle to my feet, weave and bob through the inscrutable nocturne to my open-air bedroll and collapse. Perchance to dream.

Afterword

Knee-Deep in Its Absence

OCCASIONALLY, I'M ASKED why I've chosen to make my career (so-called) writing about nature.

The answer is easy: I *have* no choice; it's in my genes. As it may just be in yours.

The best scientific guess is that crude, "proto" language first appeared among the progenitors of our species more than two million years ago. Full, "true" language, it is thought, evolved no earlier than one hundred thousand and no later than forty thousand years ago, exactly in synch with the triumphant emergence of *Homo sapiens sapiens*. (Coincidental? Not likely. The ability to communicate intricate thoughts no doubt gave early *H. s. sap* a survival edge over his less eloquent contemporary, *H. s. neandertalensis*; and in evolutionary competition between two species vying for the same niche, an edge is often enough.)

At that time and until the most recent moment of human history, our hunter-gatherer ancestors had no cultivated crops, no domesticated livestock, no industry beyond local, small-scale production of artful implements of stone, bone (including antler and horn) and wood. And since we also had no writing, all accumulated knowledge—social and religious values, tribal and family histories, myth, law, legend, ritual, *everything*—had to be precisely memorized and orally transmitted from generation to generation. And what better vehicle for organizing, condensing, memorizing and transferring the spoken word, than ... story.

Which is to say: For the overwhelming bulk of human history on this lovely earth, *our* nature was inseparable from wild nature; we *were* wild nature. It follows naturally that the characters who breathed life into ancestral story would have taken (and in surviving primitive cultures, continue to take) the form of animals, animal-humans, animal-gods, even (as in Navajo creation myth) animated landscapes.

Only about ten thousand years ago did we begin to tame wild flora and fauna, gradually trading spear, atlatl and digging stick for plow and shepherd's crook, thus biting the apple of nonsustainable technology and initiating our self-eviction from the Eden of pristine nature. In due time came industry, that irresistible magnet for urban growth. Thus, only in the last micro-second of human history has so-called progress insidiously separated the majority of humanity from daily association first with wild, then pastoral nature.

Simultaneous with and due to this estrangement, the ancestral literature of nature and place that had thrived for countless millennia began to fall out of use, out of favor, being replaced first in oral tradition, then—beginning some thirty-five hundred years ago with the invention of the first complex alphabets—in written literature. Supplanting nature was story focused ever more on an increasingly human-constructed world. In the second half of the fifteenth century, Gutenberg's printing press appeared, facilitating and speeding that sad transition.

But all that riseth returneth to earth, and now, in this living generation, as we witness the last remnants of wild nature being clear-cut, bulldozed, blacktopped and otherwise "improved" into extinction, as the spiritual quality of our lives atrophies while our material "standard of living" continues to bloat, nature-story is recapturing its deeply historical popularity and significance. Literate, thinking readers are increasingly expressing what may well be a genetic craving for nature-based story, story that reconnects us to our ancestral roots and rejoins us, at least in spirit, with the natural world that was and is our only home; story which, like religion, gives direction and meaning to our increasingly complex lives and offers hope for the future by embracing values from our pre-agricultural past.

Consequently and by and large, the character of the place in which a nature writer lives and works (or longs to return to) colors his or her work. For Wendell Berry it's rural Kentucky, for Terry Tempest Williams the Great Basin and Colorado Plateau, for Richard Nelson it's coastal Alaska, for Ann Zwinger and Edward Abbey the entire Southwest, for Bud Guthrie the Big Sky of Montana, for John Nichols the *Milagro* country around Taos.

My own place—it should be clear by now—is here in the southern Rockies. I thrive on the crisp clean air and cold clear water, the breath-sucking beauty of the creased and crenulated landscape and its abundant wildlife, the relative quiet and solitude and the personal freedom it all adds up to. *These* are the things to value most in life. It follows that these are also the things I am compelled to write about. In my case at least, the nature of the place has become the nature of the man, of the writer.

∞

During the first few years Caroline and I lived in these sublime San Juans, we had a most pleasant habit of walking or snowshoeing a mile down the mountain to spend Sunday mornings lazing around an antique wood stove drinking coffee and chatting with an octogenarian rancher friend named Helen.

Helen has spent her entire long life on the verdant riverside spread where she was born in 1905. She is living local history and a captivating storyteller. Among my favorites is her tale of the Naked Fat Man.

In the summer of 1913, when Helen was eight, her father went hunting up the tight little creek valley where my hillside cabin now squats. There, "in blow-down timber so thick you couldn't ride a horse through," Helen's father killed an exceptionally large bear that could have been the dead-last grizzly in the neighborhood. With helping hands and horses, the hunter wrestled the bruin home and hoisted it by the hind legs into a sturdy tree, then skinned it in preparation for butchering. (Few country folk in those lean and pragmatic days wasted fresh meat of any kind, and "woods pork" was widely considered a delicacy.)

It was then, with the bare bear hanging there and her father standing beside it, bloody knife in hand, that young Helen wandered into the scene. Horrified at what she saw, she burst into tears and fled. Eighty years later, Helen laughed when she recalled how that flayed bear "looked like a naked fat man hanging there. I thought Dad had killed somebody and was fixing to cut him up and feed him to us. I haven't been able to stomach bear meat since."

☙

Story spawns story.

Some years ago, while exploring a secluded aspen grove a few miles up the mountain from my cabin, I stumbled upon a hidden spring. Abundant spoor announced that deer, elk, bears, turkeys and other wildlife visited the place regularly to drink from the little pool, to browse the lush vegetation watered by the pool's brief overflow and, I like to think, just to be there.

Shadowy and quiet and a little spooky at twilight, the place exudes a preternatural ambience. Since that day, I've visited this sylvan shrine often; it has become my local refuge from Babylon. And among the most significant elements of the spirit of this special place are its bear trees: across the decades, the soft white skins of several of the larger aspens ringing the spring have collected hundreds of blackened bear-claw scars.

This in itself is hardly unique. I've seen scores of bruin-scarred aspens near dozens of secluded spring pools throughout the Rockies. Most often, it's cubs that do the climbing and whose needle-sharp claws scratch and gouge the impressionable bark, leaving distinctive curved parallel signatures. As the aspens grow, these modest tracks harden, blacken, stretch and swell, eventually coming to look as if they were made by the most monstrous of bruins.

But two ancient, special aspens near my spring wear a different sort of signature entirely: heavy, widely spaced vertical claw marks more than a foot long and at just the right height, allowing for eight decades of subsequent growth, to suggest that a very large bear once stood upright, stretched as high as possible and raked its claws heavily downward. Exactly as grizzlies are wont to do.

In step with my old friend Helen, those storybook aspens have survived nearly a century rooted firmly in this cloistered San Juan pocket. I find it a deeply poignant experience to sit quietly in that enchanted refugium and study those crude autographs and imagine them being inscribed by Helen's Naked Fat Man himself.

On one of the last occasions Caroline and I went to visit Helen, I found myself admitting to her that I was terribly envious of the simple, self-sufficient, quietly satisfying life she'd known growing up and living on a working ranch in the good old days of a still-wild West. "I'd give anything," I confessed, "to have lived your life."

"Hell," Helen snorted, "you can *have* my life. I wish I'd been born fifty years sooner." Surprised, I asked why.

"So I wouldn't be here today to see what the sonsabitches are doing to this place."

WHAT BUDDHA MIGHT SAY IF HE WERE HERE TODAY
In the forest
walk, sit, see.
Inhale ... silence.
Exhale ... solace.
At the forest's edge
live
unobtrusively
without pretense or harm.

As my old friend A. B. Guthrie, Jr., was inclined to say—the thing you've got to watch out for with progress is that there's no turning back.

Helen is past ninety now and no longer guides hunters and fishers into the wilderness or plants a big garden or keeps chickens by the score or hauls hay out to feed snow-stranded cattle or drives a horse-drawn sleigh thirteen miles to town in winter blizzards. No more grizzlies in the neighborhood either. Instead, we have ever more care-less destroyers everywhere. Ever more new roads slicing like daggers into the shrinking heart of wildness. Ever more urban refugees arriving to build ever more houses along those new roads. My magical bear trees are in mortal danger of being "harvested" for the polluting pulp mill that makes the waferboard used to build those houses. Wal-Mart is coming.

The thought of what was here once and is gone forever will not leave me as long as I live. It is as though I walk knee-deep in its absence.

Wendell Berry said that, and I live it with him daily.

Standard advice to aspiring writers is "Write about what you know." For aspiring nature writers, I'd refine that to "write about what you know and *love*."

Why do I choose to write about nature?

I *have* no choice: it's in my genes … and in my heart.

Acknowledgments

THE AUTHOR (SIC) is deeply indebted to the reckless editors of the stellar periodicals in whose pages *The Nearby Faraway* slouched—an article, an essay, a narrative at a time—toward ultimate coherence (in both senses of both words): *Backpacker, Bugle, Empire, Northern Lights, Orion, The San Juan Almanac* and *Western American Literature*. Blessings on you, one and all.

Special thanks to Henry Holt and Company for allowing me to rent back a bit of my *Ghost Grizzlies*.

And thank you Caroline Petersen, Clarke Abbey, Branson Reynolds, Bruce Woods, George Hassan, Ann Zwinger, Red Bird, Tom Shealey, Nancy Portera, Stephen Topping and Carl Brandt for your invaluable gifts of friendship and support.

Finally, to Edward Abbey, who urged me in this direction a decade ago and whose lively spirit lurks among these pages ... we have not forgot.